Workshops
in
cognitive
processes

Workshops in cognitive processes

A. Bennett
S. Hausfeld
R.A. Reeve
J. Smith

Routledge & Kegan Paul
London, Boston and Henley

This edition first published in Great Britain
and the United States of America in 1981
by Routledge & Kegan Paul Ltd
39 Store Street, London WC1E 7DD
9 Park Street, Boston, Mass. 02108, USA and
Broadway House, Newtown Road,
Henley-on-Thames, Oxon RG9 1EN
Set in IBM Press Roman 10 on 11 pt
and printed in Great Britain by
T.J. Press (Padstow) Ltd, Cornwall

ISBN 0-7100-0932-1

Contents

Contents vii

Preface to the first edition

In 1976, in an introductory Cognitive Processes course at Macquarie University, we instituted what we called 'workshops' into the laboratory programme. They proved to be so successful that we have collected the material into this manual for use by students in this and similar courses. Our course is given in the second year of psychology, following a first-year general psychology course.

The aim of the workshops is to give students an opportunity to find out at first hand about some cognitive processes. Each student chooses a workshop and then conducts an experiment on the other members of the class, collecting results and leading the discussion on the topic being investigated. We have found that involving all the students in this way facilitates understanding and discussion. Student evaluation at the end of the 1976 course showed an almost unanimous verdict that the workshops were valuable and interesting.

The equipment required for the workshops has been kept as simple as possible. In keeping with the general aim, students' involvement in making their stimuli and assembling apparatus has been encouraged. Timing devices such as chronoscopes or stop watches are used fairly frequently. A tachistoscope can be used for presenting material for short durations, but a shutter device attached to a projector could be substituted. For each workshop students can be encouraged to use their ingenuity in assembling their equipment, with the tutor on hand for guidance when needed.

The topics in the manual fall into five broad sections and can be used in conjunction with a textbook such as D. A. Norman's *Memory and Attention* (Wiley, 1976). Because topics in cognitive development are traditionally covered in courses other than cognitive processes we have omitted developmental topics, but have tried to give broad coverage to adult cognitive processing.

We hope other staff and students find the workshops as useful and stimulating as we have. We would be interested to hear user comments on any of the workshops.

We should point out that we have all contributed equally to the development of each of these workshops and the listing of authors is alphabetical rather than being intended to reflect degree of contribution.

x   *Preface to the first edition*

We would like to thank our colleagues, in particular, Peter van Sommers, Jacqueline Goodnow and Rob Hall for their encouragement and advice. Peter van Sommers also designed the cover.

We would also like to thank Anne Daubney for her help and willingness in typing our draft and final manuscript.

Adrienne Bennett
Steven Hausfeld
Robert A. Reeve
Jacqui Smith

Macquarie University
August 1977

Preface to the second edition

Since 1977 there have been significant developments in cognitive research. We have tried to incorporate some of these in a substantial revision. Although, in most cases, the original ideas for the main workshops have been retained, the Alternatives sections have been expanded to include some reference to these new developments and hopefully, to anticipate future changes. In addition, one new workshop has been introduced to each section.

The revision was also prompted by our added experience in running the workshops, by the desire to provide our own and other students with a more up-to-date text, and by the review written about our first edition by Wayne Wickelgren (*Contemporary Psychology*, 1979, vol. 24).

Adrienne Bennett
Steven Hausfeld
Robert A. Reeve
Jacqui Smith

Macquarie University
December 1980

Guide to the workshops

Each workshop has two titles: one contains the psychological terms for the area or the problem and the other sets out the problem in a more everyday way. We have tried to avoid a 'cookbook' approach for which students simply fill in the numbers. The workshops are presented as problems to be investigated, providing a number of choices to be thought about by the student. We have therefore deliberately used only the heading *General procedure* in each one (rather than the usual journal headings of *Method*, *Apparatus*, etc.), to maintain flexibility in setting out the choices facing the student in finding answers to the question asked. Students can use the journal format later in writing a report on their workshop.

At the end of each workshop there is a section headed Alternatives. The ideas in this section expand on the basic problem and in many cases pose more difficult issues to investigate. We have included these to increase the relevance of the manual to students in more advanced courses.

References have been kept to a minimum — usually only three or four articles or chapters. They are not necessarily the most recent work available in the area, but have been chosen as good representatives of a topic or point of view which has had an impact on research and theory. We expect all students running a workshop to read the main References, and those attempting any of the Alternatives to read the additional References for Alternatives.

Our experience suggests that where laboratory sessions are two hours long, one hour can be used for testing and one hour for discussion, although this can be varied, e.g. by having two short workshops for one hour each. If sessions were of one hour, data could be collected in one week and discussed in the next. The procedure used at Macquarie for two-hour sessions has been outlined below as a guide to other users; it can, of course, be varied to suit different course structures.

Students are asked at the beginning of the course to choose a workshop they would like to carry out. They can prepare their workshop either in small groups (of two or three students) or individually. (Some of the workshops are more suited to being run as a group effort, with students later writing their own reports of the experiment.) They are then assigned a particular session during the course, in which they will take over the proceedings and conduct their workshop.

The general instructions to students include the suggestions that before their laboratory session they consult their tutor at least once and that they run some pilot subjects to make sure that the testing will not take longer than will be available and that apparatus and procedure are satisfactory. It is also mentioned that student experimenters need to remember, when leading the discussion to their session, that the other students will not know much about the topic apart from what they have seen in the experiment. In fact, it is a good idea for a number of the workshops that students do not look at them in detail before they act as subjects so that the experiment may run more successfully with naive participants. However, they can be asked to read the workshop and the main References before the discussion session.

We have also used these workshops with students enrolled in extramural courses on cognitive processes. Such students typically receive taped lectures and work without regular contact with staff, except at intensive two- or three-day vacation schools. The general principles for use of the workshops by these students are the same as outlined above for regular students. It is still important for these extramural students to check their design with a tutor. They can conduct their pilot experiment on subjects available to them, and when they attend a vacation school they can test their fellow students and conduct the workshop in the same way that regular students do.

We ask all students to write a short report on their workshop in the usual journal format. Because of the small sample sizes we do not insist on significance testing and allow students simply to discuss descriptive statistics, often best presented graphically. However when the workshops are used with more advanced students, the aspects of experimental design and analysis can readily be brought into greater prominence.

I

Introduction
to
cognition

Introduction to cognition
Comprehending comprehension

This workshop is not included in a specific subject area because its aim is to introduce you to the topics and experimental methods of cognitive psychology. For this reason its format is a little different from later workshops. Your tutor may present this workshop to give you an extra indication of how to run a workshop session.

Cognitive psychologists are interested in the events which occur between the presentation of a stimulus and the performance of a response. The problem is not an easy one — that of trying to specify and measure the events and processes occurring inside people's heads.

Contemporary cognitive psychology often draws on an analogy made between the human subject and the information processing occurring within a computer. Thus many of the cognitive models you will encounter are called information-processing models. Although this analogy has problems, it does clarify some of the ways psychological problems are tackled. Both the human subject and the computer receive input, modify it, and finally produce an output after several different stages of internal processing.

To demonstrate some of these internal processes, this workshop is in two parts: Part A describes an experiment based on work by Bransford and Johnson (1972), and Part B includes discussion points on cognitive processes, using illustrations from this experiment.

Part A: A cognitive processing experiment

The workshop will follow Experiment 1 of Bransford and Johnson (1972, pp. 718-20). This experiment examined how important it is for subjects to have a suitable context in order to comprehend a prose passage.

The experimenter will need a prose passage containing some twelve to twenty simple ideas, and a corresponding picture. The passage could be Bransford and Johnson's or it could be another passage which is also expressed somewhat obliquely, so that it is very difficult to comprehend without its corresponding picture, but relatively easy with the picture.

Two groups of subjects will be used. One (context before) group will be allowed to study the picture for about a minute. The other (no context) group will not even be aware the picture exists. Both groups will then be asked to listen carefully to the passage, which the experimenter can read or play from a recording. They will be asked to try to comprehend the passage and to remember it for later recall. After listening to the passage, both groups will rate the passage for comprehension on a seven-point scale such as Bransford and Johnson used. They will then try to write down as many ideas from the passage as they can. (Scoring is easier if subjects are asked to write each idea on a new line.)

Subjects can score each other's recall protocols from a pre-prepared list of the ideas in the passage. Scoring should be fairly lenient because it is only recall of ideas that is of interest, not verbatim recall. Do subjects in the 'context before' group recall more than those in the 'no context' group? Do the groups differ in their comprehension of the passage?

The procedure above could be modified by using some of the other conditions described by Bransford and Johnson, e.g., a 'context after' or a 'partial context' group. If subject numbers permit, more than two groups could be used.

Part B: Cognitive processes involved in the task

This experimental task, like the others in this manual, involves many important cognitive processes:

1 *Attention*
   As you listen to the passage you are probably unaware of the extraneous noises in the background, the movements made by the experimenter and many other stimuli impinging on you at the time. Cognitive psychologists say that you are selectively attending to the message and suggest that you cannot attend in detail to more than one source of information at once.

2 *Pattern recognition*
   You analyse the sound patterns of the speech by breaking it into units and recognising it as a series of words organised into grammatical sentences. Additionally, you readily analyse and recognise the various patterns in the drawing. You are not only able to recognise the shapes, but you are also able to see the three-dimensional spatial relations represented by them.

3 *Short-term memory*
   As the latter half of a sentence is being read you are storing the first half of the message, in order to comprehend later the meaning of the whole sentence. To do this you must be using some sort of short-term memory.

4 *Long-term memory*
   Listening to the passage, you recognise and classify the sound patterns according to phonological, grammatical and semantic information you

have in long-term memory. You understand the drawing on the basis of material that is also stored in long-term memory.

Furthermore you may store the passage in a long-term episodic memory so that after a week or two you may still be able to remember many of the ideas in the passage.

5 *Thinking*
As you hear the passage you are probably trying to link all the ideas in the passage together in a way which makes sense of them. You are really trying to solve a sort of problem.

6 *Language processing*
You had to process, comprehend and remember linguistic material (i.e. the passage). Additionally, you only knew to do this because you were able to understand and remember the verbal instructions you were given at the beginning.

The above processes are among the major areas of study in cognitive processes. It is worth noting that although this was an experiment focussing on comprehension and memory for linguistic material, all of the above processes are importantly involved in subjects' performances in the experiment. Indeed, most cognition experiments actually involve them all, although focussing on only one or other of these processes.

Some questions to discuss and ponder later

The questions below can be answered in a fairly straightforward way. But they also include some interesting complexities which deserve further thought. You might well keep them in mind as you study cognitive processes and see how many of them are clarified by the end of your course.

1 Do your results indicate any context effects? How do they compare to the Bransford and Johnson results below (adapted from Bransford and Johnson, 1972, p. 720).

	'No context' 1 Page read once	'No context' 2 Passage read twice	'Context after'	'Partial context'	'Context before'	Maximum score
Comprehension	2.30	3.60	3.30	3.70	6.10	7.00
Recall	3.60	3.80	3.60	4.00	8.00	14.00

2 What could this experiment tell you about the way we use and process language in everyday life?
3 How many people in the 'no context' group tried to find a context for the picture? How many succeeded?
4 Is imagery important in finding a context or in remembering the passage?

What sort of process is imagining? Is it thinking? Is it perceptual? Is it in any way linguistic?

5 When you recalled the passage did you recall the ideas haphazardly or did you recall them in some systematic order? Does this tell you anything about how you remembered them?

6 Is idea recall a good way to measure memory for the passage? What other measures could we use?

7 It is often said that a picture is worth a thousand words. Here the context picture does seem to convey much more information than a single title could. How do you think we manage to get so much information so quickly out of a picture?

8 In developing a context for the passage we seem to use our entire knowledge of the world to decide what is possible in the way of a context. If we do need to process such encyclopaedic information to comprehend a short passage, what problems does this pose for a cognitive theory of language comprehension?

Reference

Bransford, J. D., and Johnson, M. K. Contextual prerequisites for understanding: Some investigations of comprehension and recall. *Journal of Verbal Learning and Verbal Behavior*, 1972, **11**, 717–26.

II

Memory

Introduction

Memory is an integral part of each of the areas covered in this book. However, it is an aspect of human behaviour which has been mostly ignored until relatively recently. The work of Bartlett (1932) still stands as a high point in the study of memory as indicated by his influence on current research. With the increasing dominance of Behaviourism in the 1930s, Bartlett's work, and memory research, was largely forgotten for the next thirty years. The concept of memory was too mentalistic for the behaviourists, who considered it outside the realm of empirical test.

It was only in the early to mid 1960s that cognitive theory generally and the study of memory in particular enjoyed a revival. At this time memory research was heavily influenced by two approaches: computer simulation models of man and the verbal learning tradition of the neo-behaviourists. Computer simulation approaches directed researchers to investigate the structure of memory, and the verbal learning approach was influential in the choice of materials with which the structure of memory would be probed (e.g. words and nonsense syllables). In your reading on the study of memory, you will undoubtedly encounter terms such as 'short-term store', 'long-term store' and 'iconic memory'. Investigating the number and the capacities of such stores was the major research aim of those influenced by the above approaches.

The dissatisfaction arising from the restrictions of these early 'box-models' of memory is well documented in a paper by Craik and Lockhart (1972). They suggested that there was really no good reason to suppose that there are distinct memory stores, as was proposed in the 'box-model' approach. They also pointed out that a more fruitful approach might lie in focussing on the processes involved in remembering. Some useful accounts and criticisms of the approach suggested by Craik and Lockhart, as well as other topics in the area of memory, can be found in a number of recent books and articles either specifically on memory or on cognitive psychology in general: (Baddeley, 1976; Cermak and Craik, 1979; Craik, 1979; Dodd and White, 1980; Glass, Holyoak and Santa, 1979; Gruneberg, Morris and Sykes, 1978; Moates and Schumacher, 1980; Puff, 1979).

The area of memory research has expanded rapidly, with many different topics receiving emphasis. Therefore, the choice of workshops for this area has been difficult because of an embarrassment of riches. The workshops included explore different aspects of memory but basically can be divided into two categories. The first covers practical applications of memory research (Workshops M1, M2, M3 and M7). The second covers more theoretical aspects of memory (Workshops M4, M5 and M6).

Workshop M1 raises the problem of the reliability of eyewitness reports and identification parade procedures. It is well recorded in memory research that we have difficulty recalling detailed information in the exact form in which it was presented. It is only recently that this finding has been specifically raised in relation to police procedures. This workshop also serves as an introductory workshop to the area of memory because it compares and contrasts performance on two basic memory research techniques, namely, recognition and recall. Workshop M2 asks another practical question: what type of telephone numbers do we remember best? In these days of 'information-overload', questions such as this are becoming increasingly important. Workshop M3 also has practical applications. It asks how expectations guide memory strategies: for example, in the context of studying for an exam, do you study differently for an essay (recall) exam compared to a multiple choice (recognition) exam? Workshop M7 investigates several related questions about our everyday long-term memories. For example, how good are we at remembering the exact details of common objects and how good is our memory for important personal events? Further work on the practical aspects of memory can be found in Gruneberg et al. (1978).

Workshops M4 and M5 explore different theoretical views of memory, but both have useful implications for remembering. Workshop M4 is based on the levels of processing view of memory proposed by Craik and Lockhart (1972). Their view suggests that remembering is not necessarily a matter of how hard you try to remember but more a matter of what you do with the material to be remembered. However, the Alternatives section of M4 points to criticisms of this view. Workshop M5 examines the 'encoding specificity hypothesis' of Tulving and Thomson (1973). This hypothesis suggests that the retrieval aids most useful in remembering material are those present at the time of first encountering the material. Workshop M6 examines the influence of naming on what we remember having seen. The problem underlying this workshop is not new — indeed it was studied by Bartlett (1932). It is the problem of whether we actually see and thus remember just what is in the world, or whether we reconstruct our memories from fragments of information from the world rather than from copies.

It was pointed out earlier that memory is an integral part of each of the areas studied in this book. Bartlett (1932) repeatedly maintained that it would be wrong to isolate any cognitive process and, in particular, memory. In studying these memory workshops you should not ignore other cognitive processes.

References

Baddeley, A. D. *The Psychology of Memory*. New York: Basic Books, 1976.
Bartlett, F. C. *Remembering*. Cambridge: Cambridge University Press, 1932.
Cermak, L. S., and Craik, F. I. M. (eds). *Levels of Processing in Human Memory*. Hillsdale, N.J.: Lawrence Erlbaum, 1979.
Craik, F. I. M. Human memory. *Annual Review of Psychology*, 1979, **30**, 63–102.
Craik, F. I. M., and Lockhart, R. S. Levels of processing: A framework for memory research. *Journal of Verbal Learning and Verbal Behavior*, 1972, **11**, 671–84.
Dodd, D. H., and White, R. M. *Cognition: Mental Structures and Processes*. Boston: Allyn & Bacon, 1980.
Glass, A. L., Holyoak, K. J., and Santa, J. L. *Cognition*. Reading, Mass.: Addison-Wesley, 1979.
Gruneberg, M. M., Morris, P. E., and Sykes, R. N. (eds). *Practical Aspects of Memory*. London: Academic Press, 1978.
Moates, D. R., and Schumacher, G. M. *An Introduction to Cognitive Psychology*. Belmont, Calif.: Wadsworth, 1980.
Puff, R. (ed.). *Memory Organization and Structure*. New York: Academic Press, 1979.
Tulving, E., and Thomson, D. M. Encoding specificity and retrieval processes in episodic memory. *Psychological Review*, 1973, **80**, 352–73.

M1 Eyewitness report
How reliable are witnesses?

Can you remember the colour and type of car that you parked beside or in front of today? There are probably few people who would remember this information, even though it would be useful if you later found that your car had been damaged. Further, if you have ever made a statement to the police, you will no doubt recognise the difficulty of remaining as objective as possible, and describing exactly what you saw or heard.

In these situations we are testing the ability to recall exact and detailed information, yet in most everyday memory contexts, we only need to be able to recognise or reconstruct general features of an event. It is not often that you are required to provide a detailed description of someone you have seen or met. Indeed, if you have only seen someone at a glance, you may even have difficulty recognising them, especially if the features that you remember are that the person was female and wore spectacles, and you are asked to identify her from several other women wearing spectacles. Buckhout (1974) presents a lively discussion on the problems inherent in setting up identification parades. He suggests, for instance, that parades can only be considered fair if all the participants fit the general description of the suspect, and if the witness is not unduly pressured to make an identification.

The problem of separating fact from fiction in reports of past experiences illustrates the theory that perhaps we don't store pictures or literal copies of events, but rather, our own interpretation of what happens. Some interesting examples supporting this theory come from Loftus (1975). She examines the effect that particular questions, or even single words within a question, may have on immediate recall and subsequent long-term memory of an event. The word 'smashed', in the question 'How fast were the cars travelling when they smashed?', produces higher estimates of speed from observers than do the words 'hit' or 'collided'. These findings are particularly relevant to police and courtroom procedures.

This workshop will examine the reliability of eyewitness testimony, and the influence that particular sorts of questions have on that testimony. The events for which memory will be tested occur on a walk around an area familiar to the subjects.

General procedure

Decide on a familiar route that will provide a source of potential questions. No matter what explanation you give to the group, some subjects will probably be aware that they should try to remember as much as they can. Even so, you will find that they won't be able to recall everything.

You will need to devise a series of questions that tap factual information — items that might have been observed during the walk and could possibly be needed in an eyewitness report. For example, you might ask the colour and type of a car that was parked illegally; whether or not a light was on, or a window open, in a particular building, etc. You could also ask how 'long' the walk was (or how 'short'), together with the time at which the group passed X, or did Y. To collect the right answers for these questions you will need to go on the walk at the same time as the subjects. Perhaps a second experimenter could lead the way, as the first experimenter notes the answers.

If you vary the wording of your questions, you will be able to test whether your subjects' reports are open to the sort of bias Loftus reports. For example, subjects might estimate shorter times or distances when asked, 'How short was the walk?', than when asked how 'long' it was. You could contrast answers given by one group to a neutral question (e.g. estimate the length of time taken for the walk) with the responses of other subjects given a biased version of the same question. Loftus (1975) gives several examples of the sorts of wording changes that lead to bias effects. Simply score the proportion of correct answers and the proportion of answers given in the direction of the bias.

As well as these general observations, you could arrange for your subjects to see a particular person during the walk. This person would be a colleague, unknown to the subjects, who is involved in some inconspicuous act (for example, opening a door or standing in a corner). If you have the facilities available, arrange to have a photograph taken of the person, and of several other people also unknown to the subjects. Using these photographs, you can set up an identification parade. You will need to decide the composition of the line-up; should the people be of the same sex and of similar appearance to 'the person', or a mixture? Indeed you might decide to leave 'the person's' photograph out of the line-up, and see how many subjects still make an identification. Perhaps instructions are important in this setting too. You could state that it is not necessary to make an identification, or leave the situation ambiguous (e.g. 'look carefully and choose the person you saw').

If you are unable to obtain photographs, you might instead arrange a live identification parade, or simply ask subjects to describe the person (e.g. their height, weight, etc.). Indeed it would be interesting to compare the accuracy of descriptions people give with the accuracy of recognition. You will have to devise a way to score the descriptions. This could involve either calculating the percentage of subjects noting each feature (e.g. sex, height, weight, hair colour, clothing, etc.), or scoring, for each subject, the number of features correctly described.

When discussing your results you could consider the implications that this study, and those of Buckhout (1974) and Loftus (1975) have for police and court procedures. How would you arrange an identification parade? Are there any facial features, or aspects of appearance, that are crucial for recognition? How does asking a simple question change someone's memory of an event? Does it just alter their response (e.g. by demand characteristics) rather than change their memory? What implications does this research have for theories about recognition and recall?

Alternatives

If you have access to video or film equipment and the possibility of testing over two sessions, you could replicate either the 'Reconstruction of auto-mobile destruction' study or one of the similar studies described by Loftus (1975). In these experiments, it was found that the wording of questions asked immediately after viewing a filmed incident biased reconstruction of the incident one week later. Miller and Loftus (1976) report that subjects can even be induced to associate specific people mistakenly with particular events, through the subtle use of leading questions. You could demonstrate this effect yourself, using a slide sequence similar to Miller and Loftus or perhaps using appropriate questions to bias memory of a real-life encounter. All of these examples could have disastrous consequences in real life.

It is also interesting to consider what features of a face are important for recognition. If you were asked by a bank robber what sort of disguise is better, dark glasses, a beard or a wig, you might refer her to the paper by Patterson and Baddeley (1977). They presented subjects with several photographs to remember, then tested recognition of the same faces with changes in pose or expression, or the addition of a disguise. Further, they examined the effects of different encoding strategies by having subjects either rate each photograph on scales related to physical or personality features (Experiment 1) or learn to associate a name with each face (Experiment 2). Overall, rating personality features proved to be more effective than rating physical features.

Should you choose to replicate either of their experiments, you might note that Patterson and Baddeley used only female subjects. If you are not familiar with the signal detection analysis used by these researchers, you could simply keep a separate record of hits and false-alarms. What are the implications that the results have for the use of Identikit pictures? Perhaps you might also test whether an Identikit picture is easily recognised as a representation of a previously seen picture of a real face. Here again, you could investigate the effects of disguises on recognition.

You might also test whether familiarity with the person behind the face influences ease of recognition. If you are familiar with the person, then you may well recognise them regardless of any pose, particular facial expression or disguise they adopt. Indeed, with people we know well, we often do not specifically notice additions like spectacles or a new hairstyle. Another important aspect of the Patterson and Baddeley study was the encoding strategy effects that they report. What do these suggest about ways of trying to remember faces and names, when you are being introduced to people?

References

Buckhout, R. Eyewitness testimony. *Scientific American*, 1974, **231** (6), 23–31 (Offprint No. 562).

Loftus, E. F. Leading questions and the eyewitness report. *Cognitive Psychology*, 1975, 7, 560–72.

References for Alternatives

Miller, D. G., and Loftus, E. F. Influencing memory for people and their actions. *Bulletin of the Psychonomic Society*, 1976, 7, 9–11.

Patterson, K. E., and Baddeley, A. D. When face recognition fails. *Journal of Experimental Psychology: Human Learning and Memory*, 1977, 3, 406–17.

M2 Memory for numbers

What form of telephone numbers would we remember best?

A number of things we see and use every day have been developed with the help of psychological research. Post-codes and telephone numbers, for example, need to be in a form that is easy to remember. Results from experiments on human memory can assist in deciding about the form and sequence of such numbers. For example, what is the most efficient format for telephone numbers — all numbers, all digits, letters plus digits? Efficiency is achieved by some compromise between the number of combinations required and the load on memory. Broadbent (1971) discusses how this problem was solved for the British post-code system by examining experimental evidence on ease of memory for different digit-letter groupings.

How would we go about obtaining evidence to decide on the form for telephone numbers? One way is to test subjects' memory for lists of certain types of items. Psychologists have devoted considerable time and effort over the years to studying this sort of memory. Norman (1976) sets out the history of this work, including George Miller's concept of 'the magical number seven plus or minus two'. This concept refers to the limit of about seven items on the immediate memory span for unconnected material. Norman points out how we can remember more items by grouping or coding the items into 'chunks'.

A second method of obtaining evidence is to attempt a closer replication of the actual way telephone numbers are usually used, i.e. singly, and with reference to a name. The experiment described for this workshop uses the first method, with the second as an alternative.

General procedure

This workshop compares subjects' memory for three types of items: those with 7 digits, 7 letters and 7 letters with digits. You will need a number of examples of each type, say twelve, and could present half of each type in a grouped form (e.g., 654-2685, or TRD-KHSI, or TRJ-5447) and the other half in an ungrouped form (e.g., 3874255, or BKHITDR, or BKJ4258). Each subject would be tested for memory of each of the six types of item, gaining a score in each cell of the design set out below:

	All digits	All letters	Mixed
Grouped			
Ungrouped			

This constitutes a 2 × 3 factorial design with repeated measures on both factors.

The lists can be presented using an overhead projector, or in a booklet which is covered up after the subject has inspected a list so that recall of sequences can be tested. You could also consider aural presentation.

The factors you will need to think about and whose effects you can perhaps test within your experiment, or in a pilot experiment, are

(i) the number of sequences in each list;
(ii) how long to allow subjects to study each list; and
(iii) the retention interval, i.e. the time between the end of the last sequence to be shown and the request to write down the items recalled.

It is probably easier for scoring purposes to present all the lists of the same type of sequence together, i.e. 'pure' lists, rather than 'mixed' or randomised lists. You would then need to control for the possibility of practice effects (the improvement of memory performance for lists presented later), by randomising the order of list presentation so that each subject receives the lists in a different order. You will have to decide whether to score sequences as a whole, the individual digits, or digits in positions.

Means for each cell can be calculated from subjects' scores and the results graphed. You can see whether grouping made any difference overall and which form of item was remembered most successfully. Discussion could profitably include introspective reports from your subjects on how they did the task. You could consider the points which Broadbent (1971) raises in relation to English 'zip codes' and telephone numbers. For example, do people make more mistakes for letters and digits in the middle of each sequence? How relevant do you think the experimental design used in this workshop is to the question being asked? Can you see any improvements in it now that you have carried it out?

Alternatives

Broadbent (1971) suggests that area prefixes for telephone numbers can aid memory. You could check this by comparing memory for random numbers with memory for some telephone numbers from your city or country. You could group the area prefixes separately from the rest of the number or present the whole number ungrouped.

As mentioned in the introduction, another way of obtaining data on the most efficient format for telephone numbers is to try to simulate the procedures and times normally involved in the storage and retrieval of these numbers in daily life. You will need to use your ingenuity here. One suggestion is to use some variant of a paired-associates design, i.e. presenting surnames paired with different types of numbers.

As already discussed, chunking of items for memory may be important in designing number sequences, e.g. telephone numbers. Ericsson, Chase, and Faloon (1980) report a very interesting experiment in which, by learning to use complex chunking strategies, one person was able to recall up to 79 random digits. If you have time to train one or two people (perhaps even yourself) over a shorter period than Ericsson *et al.* used, you might gain some valuable insights into the potential of such chunking strategies.

The subject in Ericsson *et al.* coded the digits into three- or four-digit chunks. Broadbent (1975) reviews several studies suggesting that three to four is closer to the short-term memory processing limit. You might like to follow up some of his ideas.

References

Broadbent, D. E. Relation between theory and application in psychology. In P. B. Warr (ed.). *Psychology at Work*. Harmondsworth: Penguin, 1971.

Norman, D. A. *Memory and Attention: An Introduction to Human Information Processing* (2nd edn). New York: Wiley, 1976.

References for Alternatives

Broadbent, D. E. The magical number seven after fifteen years. In A. Kennedy & A. Wilkes (eds). *Studies in Long Term Memory*. London: John Wiley, 1975.

Ericsson, K. A., Chase, W. G., and Faloon, S. Acquisition of a memory skill. *Science,* 1980, **208**, 1181–2.

M3 Test appropriate strategies for recall and recognition

How do expectations guide memory?

Imagine yourself preparing for an exam. You know that half the exam will be multiple-choice type questions and the other half essays. Do you try and prepare for the two halves differently? Do you or can you adjust your learning strategies to meet the sort of test you expect? Answers to these questions have been sought in experimental studies which investigated how people deal with free-recall and recognition memory tests — memory tests which closely parallel the requirements of essay writing and multiple-choice tests, respectively.

Many memory researchers consider that recall and recognition reflect two qualitatively distinct psychological processes. It is argued that the storage of verbal associations may be more critical for recall than recognition. By contrast, simple item repetition or rehearsal results in efficient recognition performance but in poor recall. General support for these claims is gathered from experiments which demonstrate that leading subjects to expect a certain type of memory test, but actually giving them a different test, results in a decrement in performance. That is, when expectations are violated, memory performance is adversely affected, because it would seem subjects adopt test-appropriate encoding strategies.

Hall, Grossman and Elwood (1976), in a series of experiments, examined the relationship between the way relatively unrelated words are encoded for recall and for recognition. Their basic paradigm involved subjects memorising lists of words. After an interval they either had to recall or recognise the words. For the first three lists, subjects knew the nature of the memory test. However, on the fourth trial some subjects had a different test from the one they expected.

The results of Hall *et al.*'s experiments indicate that test appropriate encoding is especially important for recall memory tests. A rather interesting finding in this experiment emerges from subjects' self-reports. Hall *et al.* asked subjects to rate on a seven-point scale the degree to which they used eleven encoding strategies in their preparation for the test. They found that the critical encoding differences produced by manipulating test expectancy were quantitative rather than qualitative in nature. That is subjects' ratings indicated that they used similar kinds of encoding strategies when preparing for recall and recognition tests. This finding is counter to the view expressed above that recall and recognition reflect two qualitatively distinct psychological processes.

This workshop involves a partial replication of either Experiment 1 or 2 outlined by Hall *et al*. Their experiments were designed to investigate a number of variables which were thought to interact with test expectancy (e.g. free study versus paced study and short-study time versus long-study time). These variables can be held constant for this workshop and only the expectancy effects themselves will be examined.

This workshop is based on a 2 X 2 factorial design with independent groups (i.e. two encoding treatments: recall and recognition; and two test treatments: recall and recognition).

General procedure

You need to decide which experiment of Hall *et al*. you will follow. In their first experiment, subjects' test expectations were met on the first three memory test trials with an unexpected type of memory test on the fourth trial. In their second experiment, there were no set-inducing trials preceding the critical memory test. You can get your list of unrelated nouns for the experiment from Paivio, Yuille and Madigan's (1968) word norms. You will need to construct test booklets to test for either or both recall and recognition. It is important that your subjects do not find out about the nature of the experiment until it is over.

Hall *et al*. used fairly short lists, which resulted in ceiling effects in the recognition phase of their experiment. You could use longer lists. You will also need to decide on the nature of the distractors used in the recognition set. Both of these factors, list length and type of distractors, were important in the pattern of results obtained in the Hall *et al*. study.

Following the final test, all subjects could complete a questionnaire concerning their strategies. The format of such a questionnaire is contained in Hall *et al*. (p. 508). Did test expectancy influence the type of strategies used?

It would be inappropriate to analyse your data fully (e.g. by analysis of variance) because it is unlikely you will have sufficient numbers in the cells to make such an analysis meaningful. Inspection of the appropriate cell means and a graphing of these should be sufficient to indicate major trends in the data.

In discussion, you could consider whether your results support a qualitative or a quantitative distinction between recognition and recall. Because subjects' self-reports are notoriously unreliable, you could also discuss how further to investigate the qualitative view.

Alternatives

Alternatives have already been mentioned above, e.g. altering the length of the to-be-remembered word lists, and also examining the nature of the distractor set in the recognition phase. The second of these alternatives seems important because it is asserted (Conner, 1977) that the difference between recall and recognition lies in the fact that the 'associativeness' of items is unimportant for encoding in recognition, but is important for recall. If this is the case, then the nature of the distractor set should not affect recognition performance.

Conner (1977) has investigated this alternative in a slightly different way. She argued that the nature of the initial list organisation should be crucial for recall, but not for recognition. In her experiment she manipulated the list organisation variable in several ways, in addition to violating subjects' memory test expectations. Conner's manipulations might be a worthwhile inclusion or control in your experiment.

References

Hall, J. W., Grossman, L. R., and Elwood, K. D. Differences in encoding for free recall vs. recognition. *Memory & Cognition*, 1976, **4**, 507-13.

Paivio, A., Yuille, J. C., and Madigan, S. Concreteness, imagery and meaningfulness values for 925 nouns. *Journal of Experimental Psychology Monograph Supplement*, 1968, **76**, 1-25.

Reference for Alternatives

Conner, J. M. Effects of organization and expectancy on recall and recognition. *Memory & Cognition*, 1977, **5**, 315-18.

M4 Levels of processing
It's not how hard you try but what you do

Nearly everybody is confronted with the problem of how to remember information efficiently. For example, is it best simply to repeat the to-be-remembered information over to yourself or is it better to employ a more complex learning strategy such as the mnemonics we learned at school? Recent memory research has thrown some light on these issues. Craik and Lockhart (1972) suggested that it is not necessarily the intent to remember *per se* that is important, but rather how we process the information in the first place. Memory is thus seen as a by-product of the type of processing we carry out on information.

Craik and Lockhart argued that if only the physical characteristics of the information are noted or analysed when material is first seen by the subject, then it will not be very well remembered. If, on the other hand, the meaning of the material is analysed, then memory for it will increase. Support for this idea comes from incidental learning studies in which subjects were asked to make judgments about material (e.g. single words), unaware that their memory would be tested for those words. The results indicated that judgment tasks requiring 'deep', semantic processing lead to recall performance equivalent to that produced by intentional learning studies. In contrast, judgment tasks requiring 'shallow', non-semantic processing lead to poorer memory performance. It is not the intent to remember *per se* that is important, but how you process the to-be-remembered material. This statement holds equally well for studies on recognition as for studies on free-recall.

Craik and Tulving (1975), in ten experiments, explored various facets of this 'levels of processing' framework for memory research proposed by Craik and Lockhart. Subjects were induced to process words to different depths by answering questions about the words. For example, shallow encodings were achieved by asking questions about typescript; intermediate levels of encoding were accomplished by asking questions about rhymes; deep levels were induced by asking whether words would fit into a given category or sentence frame. After the encoding phase was completed, subjects were unexpectedly given a recall or recognition test. Deeper processing led to better memory performance.

It could be argued that deep encoding tasks lead to better memory because subjects spend more time on encoding for them than for shallow encoding tasks. Perhaps it is processing time which determines performance, and not the qualitative nature of the task. Craik and Tulving explored this possibility in Experiment 5, in which the shallow non-semantic task was difficult to perform and took longer than the comparison semantic task. The current workshop is based on this experiment.

General procedure

In this workshop a comparison is made between recognition memory performance of two independent groups, which are differentiated on the basis of the incidental orienting tasks they receive. One group will receive a time-consuming, shallow, non-semantic task which is difficult to perform, whilst the other group will receive an easier, but deeper, semantic task. Subjects complete the orienting tasks on a list of words without knowing they will be required to recognise the words later.

Both groups will need to be given appropriate instructions, not mentioning the fact that it is a memory experiment. Each group is tested separately. You could use the same orienting tasks as Craik and Tulving: for example, in the non-semantic task, subjects judge as quickly as possible whether a vowel/consonant pattern (e.g. CCVVC) is the correct representation of a subsequent word; and for the semantic task, subjects decide as quickly as possible whether a given word fits meaningfully into a particular sentence. Alternatively, you might like to make up your own tasks using the Craik and Tulving experiments as a guide.

The experiment requires that you record and measure the nature of your subjects' decisions as well as the latency of their responses. To achieve this they will need to work in pairs, one acting as the subject and the other recording the responses. If time permits, subject and recorder could then reverse roles and repeat the procedure with a second set of memory materials. You will need a chronoscope or a similar timing-device for each pair. Other materials needed include cards with consonant/vowel patterns on them and cards with incomplete sentences on them. You will also need a list of to-be-remembered words, a word list of confusion items for the recognition test, a response sheet for recording subjects' responses in the orienting tasks and test booklets to test for recognition memory.

The sequence of events for testing a subject is as follows: firstly, show a card with either the appropriate vowel/consonant pattern (for Group 1), or the incomplete sentence (for Group 2). Then present the word about which subjects have to make a decision. The word can either be spoken or presented on a card. Presentation of the word is the signal for the person recording the responses to start the timer. The subject stops the timer himself, simultaneously saying his decision (i.e. either 'yes' or 'no'). At the conclusion of this phase of the experiment you present the recognition memory test.

The main interest of this workshop is in whether depth of processing or time of processing is the important variable affecting memory performance. Therefore analysis of results will involve a comparison of the mean latencies for the two types of tasks for both 'yes' and 'no' responses. You will also need to compare the mean proportion of words recognised for the two types of tasks, again for both 'yes' and 'no' responses.

In discussion, you could consider whether the notion of depth of processing provides a useful approach to memory. For example, is it possible to specify *a priori* the depth of processing required by a task? You could also discuss the validity of the claim that the intent to remember *per se* is not necessarily important in remembering. You may also try to suggest why it seems that sometimes individuals remember words better if they made a positive response in the initial orienting task than if they made a negative response. Did you find this effect in your data? You could try and think of practical everyday situations where this approach to memory might prove useful.

Alternatives

There are numerous alternatives to be found among the ten experiments reported by Craik and Tulving which could form the basis of an experiment.

The levels-of-processing orientation has undoubtedly done much to stimulate memory research. Recent experimental findings, however, suggest the model needs modifying. For example, one criticism is that semantic memory measures are frequently used to test the retention of non-semantic information. This suggests that the memory test may be inappropriate in relation to the encoding task. Stein (1978) argued that this procedure spuriously confirms the view that semantic processing leads to better retention than non-semantic processing. He showed that retention of non-semantic information is not necessarily inferior to that of semantic information provided an appropriate memory test is used. Stein also demonstrated that the relative uniqueness of item encoding affects the retention of non-semantic information and to some extent semantic information. You could either replicate his experiment or see if the procedure extends to other non-semantic tasks or perhaps to non-verbal material, e.g. pictures. It might also be interesting to see whether Stein's results hold up over a longer retention interval.

Another criticism of the levels-of-processing model has been presented by Tyler, Hertel, McCullum and Ellis (1979) who argued, contrary to Craik and Tulving and our subtitle, that cognitive effort is an influential factor in memory performance. In their experiment subjects had to respond as quickly as possible to a tone at about the time they made their orienting task judgment. This allowed Tyler *et al.* to obtain an independent and more accurate index of effort than the usual measure, namely, the orienting-response latency. Their results suggested that typical levels of processing results may be contaminated by an effort factor, although they concluded that effort and levels of processing effects can be separated. It might be interesting to see if their method works for more formal (i.e. shallower) orienting tasks, such as case or colour judgments: these tasks might produce stronger levels of processing effects than Tyler *et al.* were able to find. You might also use a recognition test instead of recall. You could also consider if and how the levels of processing model has to be changed to accommodate the data presented by Tyler *et al.* and Stein.

References

Craik, F. I. M., and Lockhart, R. S. Levels of processing: A framework for memory research. *Journal of Verbal Learning and Verbal Behavior*, 1972, **11**, 671-84.

Craik, F. I. M., and Tulving, E. Depth of processing and the retention of words in episodic memory. *Journal of Experimental Psychology: General*, 1975, **104**, 268-94.

References for Alternatives

Stein, B. S. Depth of processing reexamined: The effects of the precision of encoding and test appropriateness. *Journal of Verbal Learning and Verbal Behavior*, 1978, **17**, 165-74.

Tyler, S. W., Hertel, P. T., McCullum, M. C., and Ellis, H. C. Cognitive effort and memory. *Journal of Experimental Psychology: Human Learning and Memory*, 1979, **5**, 607-17.

M5 Recognition failure of recallable items and encoding specificity

When can we recall things we can't recognise?

Most of us have, at some time, experienced an inability to recall a name or a place, but as soon as someone else has mentioned it we have immediately recognised it with an exclamation of 'Of course, that's it!' Memory researchers have supported this anecdotal evidence and have incorporated it into their theories by suggesting that recognition is easier than recall. Further, it has been suggested by some that recall consists of an internal generation of possible responses followed by a recognition operation on these self-generated items. Recognition is seen as the simplest of these two sub-processes of recall. This analysis is consistent with our intuitions that recognition is fairly immediate and is easier than recall. Students, for example, often feel that a multiple-choice (recognition) examination is easier than an essay (recall) examination.

However Watkins and Tulving (1975) discussed the body of literature, particularly the work of Tulving and Thomson, which showed some surprising examples of recall being easier than recognition. Subjects sometimes cannot recognise material they later recall. More specifically, subjects fail to *recognise* words presented in a context different from the context they were originally presented in, but these subjects are later able to *recall* the words in their original context. This result would be rather like your being unable to recognise a name when someone suggested it, even though you could actually recall it later when you returned to where you had been introduced to the name.

These findings seem contrary to the generation-recognition theories of recall which see recognition as one part of the recall process. Recognition seems to depend, like recall, on context, so that recognition is not the immediate, automatic process it once seemed. Encoded and recallable material can fail to be recognised if it is presented in a context different from that to which it was originally encoded.

Tulving and Thomson explained their findings in terms of their principle of 'encoding specificity', which suggests that the original encoding operations determine what is stored in episodic memory, hence what retrieval cues are effective. Recognition fails when the recognition context and, consequently, the available retrieval cues do not match the encoding context.

For example, if the target word 'BLACK' is initially encoded in the context of a weakly associated cue like 'train' it can subsequently fail to be recognised in the context of a strong associate like 'white', which readily elicits it. This is despite the fact that the target 'BLACK' is recalled when cued by its initial context word, 'train'.

General procedure

Following the procedure of Tulving and Thomson which Watkins and Tulving outlined in their introduction (pp. 10 ff), you will need three lists of paired associates in which each target word is capitalised (e.g. 'CHAIR') and is paired with a weakly associated cue word in lower case (e.g. 'glue'). You could use the two 24–word lists reproduced in Watkins and Tulving's paper and devise a third list of your own. You may have to consult some word-association norms for this.

Subjects will be tested on the three lists successively, with the first two lists used as practice lists to encourage subjects to encode each target word in the context of its cue word. You might follow Watkins and Tulving (Experiment 6) and try omitting one or both of these practice lists, especially if your testing time is limited.

For the first practice list, subjects will be shown the list of paired associates and told that they should remember the capitalised target words and that the associated cue words should help them to do this. The list of pairs could be presented one pair at a time, or, more easily, all at once. For this you could use printed sheets or an overhead projector, either of which would allow subjects to be tested in groups. After studying these paired-associates, subjects will be given a randomly ordered list of the cue words and asked to recall the target word associated with each cue. This cued recall procedure will be repeated for the second practice list.

The presentation of the critical third list will be as for the first two lists. However prior to the cued recall task, subjects will be given a list of strong associates, one for each target word (e.g. 'table' is a strong associate of 'CHAIR'). Subjects will then be asked to write down three or four free associates to each of these strong associates. Next they will be asked to circle any of these self-generated words which they recognise as target words from the critical list. Finally, you will give subjects the original cue words for the third list and ask them to do the standard cued recall task.

You now need to compare the mean percentage of words recalled for each of the three lists and the mean percentage of target words correctly recognised from among the subject-generated words for the last list. For each list, calculate the mean number of words recalled and convert this to a percentage. If time or facilities prohibit full scoring, then you could ignore the practice lists, concentrating on the critical third list. Next you should calculate, across all subjects, the total number of third list target words generated in free association, and the total number of these subsequently recognised. The ratio of this total number of recognised targets to the total number of generated targets is the mean proportion of targets recognised by the group. Convert this proportion to a percentage.

If time permits a fuller analysis of the results, you might see how many words were recalled but not recognised and how many were recognised but not recalled.

In discussion you can consider how far Tulving and Thomson's results can be generalised, especially in view of their unusual procedure. Watkins and Tulving, for example, argued that their 'hocus pocus' procedures are not necessary to produce the phenomenon and expressed surprise that no one had previously observed the phenomenon. Did you find that recall was easier than recognition? You could also consider what your results suggest about the nature of recall and recognition. Do you agree with the episodic or the tagging theory?

Alternatives

Because their experiment is rather unusual, it is useful to experience the full complexity of Tulving and Thomson's original design with its repeated testing of memory. If time permits, however, you could run extra treatments involving one or more of the simplifications which Watkins and Tulving introduced in their experiments.

You might use some non-associative cue words. The cue words could, for example, be related to the target words by being rhymes rather than by being weak associates. Do non-semantic cues work in the same way as semantic cues?

Most research on the encoding specificity hypothesis has used verbal materials and, as Winograd and Rivers-Bulkeley (1977) argued, it is important to extend research by using a wider range of materials. Their research on context effects on face recognition served this purpose and added to the theoretical debate about encoding specificity. Although such context effects with words might be explained in terms of semantic flexibility this cannot apply for faces. You could try to replicate Winograd and Rivers-Bulkeley's effects with faces or you could try different materials, for example, holiday slides.

Although much has been made here and in the literature of subjects' failure to recognise words they later recall, Wallace (1978) has very cleverly shown that this is just one of a series of context effects. He did find recognition failure of recallable words, but he also found recognition failure of recognisable words, and recall failure of recallable words. His point was that memory is good in the context of the encoding cue words but not in a novel context. Wallace's contribution is in showing that recognition failure of recallable words is one of several phenomena explained by cueing contexts. His paper provides several good ideas for an alternative workshop.

By looking at contexts other than cue words, you could extend Wallace's suggestion that memory is best when the encoding context is reinstated. Smith (1979), for example, looked at the effects of the context provided by the room in which learning and testing take place. Basically he found that memory is best in the original room, although memory in another room can be improved by instructions to recall the original room. It would be interesting to repeat Smith's experiment perhaps adding some variations of your own, such as a recognition rather than a recall test.

Smith also mentioned some research suggesting that one 'context' for learning can be one's pharmacological stage. This suggests that if you learn something while drunk you might not remember it as well when sober as you would when drunk again. It could be fun to investigate this suggestion, but keep in mind that the experimenters should remain sober!

Reference

Watkins, M. J., and Tulving, E. Episodic memory: When recognition fails. *Journal of Experimental Psychology: General*, 1975, **104**, 5-29.

References for Alternatives

Smith, S. M. Remembering in and out of context. *Journal of Experimental Psychology: Human Learning and Memory*, 1979, **5**, 460-71.

Wallace, W. P. Recognition failure of recallable words and recognizable words. *Journal of Experimental Psychology: Human Learning and Memory*, 1978, **4**, 441-52.

Winograd, E., and Rivers-Bulkeley, N. T. Effects of changing context on remembering faces. *Journal of Experimental Psychology: Human Learning and Memory*, 1977, **3**, 397-405.

M6 Verbal labelling and memory

How does naming affect what we remember seeing?

In a now classical study, Carmichael, Hogan and Walter (1932) demonstrated that labels given to pictures influence how the picture is reconstructed from memory. For example, one of the pictures presented by Carmichael, Hogan and Walter to their subjects was of two balls separated by a narrow bar. Some subjects were told that this line drawing was of a dumbell, while others were told it was a pair of spectacles. When asked to draw the pictures after an interval, subjects tended to draw a picture that was more consistent with the referent of the given verbal label than with the picture they had seen.

In a more recent study, Bower, Karlin and Dueck (1975) suggested that a major determinant of how well a person can remember a picture is whether or not the person understands the picture at the time of study. They pointed out that this hypothesis was derived from linguistic research which found that memory for a sentence is a function of how well it is understood. For example, a subject asked to remember the sentence 'The notes were sour because the seams split' is more likely to remember it if, at the time of presentation, a thematic prompt word such as 'bagpipe' is given. The prompt makes the sentence more meaningful and thus more likely to be remembered.

Bower *et al*. suggested that this sort of argument should also apply when people are asked to remember pictures that are hard to understand by themselves. When the pictures are presented with a verbal label which makes them meaningful, they should be more likely to be recalled.

They tested this hypothesis in experiments using nonsensical pictures called 'droodles'. In Experiment 1, subjects saw a series of droodles, with or without an accompanying verbal interpretation. They showed better recall performance, as measured by drawing, if they had received the interpretation of the pictures during their study than if they had received no interpretation. In Experiment 2, subjects studied pairs of droodles with or without a linking interpretation. Subjects who heard a phrase identifying and inter-relating the pictures of a pair showed greater cued recall and associative matching (i.e. putting the separate halves together) than subjects who received no interpretation.

This workshop is based on Experiment 2 of Bower *et al.* and aims to test the influence of labelling on associative picture memory.

General procedure

You will need to generate a set of droodles, using as a guide those shown by Bower *et al.* (pp. 217-18), and keeping in mind their comments on the relationships between the pictures (p. 219). Remember each pair needs an appropriate unifying label. Thirty such pairs should be sufficient for the experiment.

This workshop compares the memory for picture pairs of two groups of subjects: Group 1 is given a unifying label and Group 2 no label. Each group is given two types of memory test following a single presentation of the memory droodles. The first is cued recall, where the subject is shown one half of the droodle pair and is asked to draw from memory the corresponding half. The second type of memory test is associative matching, where the subject is shown all the droodle pairs at once, and has to match the corresponding pairs.

Firstly, divide your subjects into the two groups, giving each appropriate instructions about their task. You can present the droodle pairs either by holding up cards with the drawings on them, or on an overhead projector, or in booklet form with the experimenter indicating when subjects should turn the page. The last suggestion is the most efficient because it means you can test both groups simultaneously, with Group 1 having the unifying label printed in the booklet. Otherwise you will have to run the two groups separately.

In the cued recall part of the experiment, at the time of test you will be presenting one member of the droodle pair and asking the group to draw the other member. It is, therefore, a good idea to keep presentation position constant. For example, present the stimulus part of the drawing on the left and the response part on the right. Following the presentation of the droodle pairs you can proceed with the cued recall test, emphasising that the subjects need sketch only the basic outline of the drawing. This phase of the experiment would be easier if printed booklets were available with subjects working at their own pace. You could allow subjects ten minutes to complete the task.

After the completion of the cued recall task, move on to the associative matching task. Because you are group testing you will need to modify the procedure outlined in Bower *et al.* One way to do this is to give your subjects both the stimulus cards and the response cards in a pack. Your subjects' task is to match each stimulus card with a response card. Allow your subjects about ten minutes to complete this task. Then you could lay out a set of correct droodle pairs, and subjects could score their performance on both types of memory test.

Two *t*-tests would be sufficient to determine the possible statistical significance of any difference between the label group and the non-label group for the two types of memory test.

In discussion, you could consider whether you might obtain the same effects using meaningful pictures instead of droodles. Although this suggestion could form the basis of an alternative experiment, it does raise a difficult conceptual problem, namely, what makes a picture meaningful or meaningless. You could also discuss what effect the thematic prompt is having. Does it operate at the time of encoding, as claimed by Carmichael *et al.* (1932), or does it operate as a retrieval cue, or perhaps as an interaction of both? You could ask your subjects in the no-label group whether they made up their own labels. How might this affect your results? What are the implications of your results and those obtained by Bower *et al.* for a model of memory?

Alternatives

The first experiment of Bower *et al.* mentioned in the introduction is a possible alternative workshop. They interpreted their results as indicating that giving a meaning to a nonsensical picture makes it easier to store and remember later. However, as has been pointed out (Klatzky and Stoy, 1978, p. 78; Rafnel and Klatzky, 1978, p. 631), in order to check that this effect is not simply a function of labels *per se*, it is necessary to include a control condition with droodles paired with a non-appropriate label. You could investigate this as an alternative experiment and see whether you agree with their conclusion that it is only meaningful labels provided at encoding which lead to superior recall.

Rafnel and Klatzky further analysed the facilitating effect of labelling (or semantic interpretation) by seeing whether it occurs because of superior storage of the physical and/or of the semantic properties of the picture. Rafnel and Klatzky argued that their findings showed that labelling leads to superior semantic memory. However, their results are not consistent across experiments or even within experiments across response measures, and their sequencing of statistical tests is questionable. Nevertheless, their idea of using a recognition test with physical- and semantic-change distractors is worth pursuing. You could explore further whether their pattern of data would be altered if the non-semantic change were always readily detectable and clearly made to the form described by the label. The example in their Figure 1 (p. 635) shows a 'physical-change' distractor in which the physical detail changed is relatively minor. Remember that any physical change here should not produce a semantic change.

The semantic-physical distinction was also discussed by Klatzky and Stoy (pp. 71–2) in their more general analysis of semantic effects on visual processing. They reported research using a different paradigm, namely, subjects making judgments about the physical or semantic identity of pairs of stimuli. The effects of naming an object are seen in their category-structure effect. Klatzky and Stoy's analysis of research lead them to the conclusion that purely visual processing is a rare event. You could consult their work for ideas for further alternative experiments which include studies of the effect of names and structures of categories on memory for the visual appearance of objects.

References

Bower, G. H., Karlin, M. B., and Dueck, A. Comprehension and memory for pictures. *Memory & Cognition*, 1975, **3**, 216-20.

Carmichael, L., Hogan, H. P., and Walter, A. A. An experimental study of the effect of language on the reproduction of visually perceived form. *Journal of Experimental Psychology*, 1932, **15**, 73-83.

References for Alternatives

Klatzky, R. L., and Stoy, A. M. Semantic information and visual information processing. In J. W. Cotton & R. L. Klatzky (eds). *Semantic Factors in Cogniton.* Hillsdale, New Jersey: Lawrence Erlbaum Associates, 1978.

Rafnel, K. J., and Klatzky, R. L. Meaningful-interpretation effects on codes of nonsense pictures. *Journal of Experimental Psychology: Human Learning and Memory*, 1978, **4**, 631-46.

M7 Long-term memory for common objects and events

Does your memory have an eye for detail?

Most people feel that they can remember frequently encountered objects quite accurately. However, if you actually ask them to draw, in detail, the design from a dollar note, the face of a telephone dial, or the information on their student identity card, then you will probably find that they are not as accurate as they thought. (Stop reading for a moment and try these examples for yourself). They are examples of everyday things which, although apparently readily recognised, are often difficult to recall. Such gaps in our memory are surprising considering the extent of our experience with the objects. These gaps are also in sharp contrast to the fact that we do seem to remember a large number of trivial and not-so-trivial bits of information. For example, we remember important telephone numbers, where we went on our last holiday, that milk comes from cows and that rain is wet, where we live and sufficient information to be able to discriminate cats from dogs. We also seem to have very good and often vivid memories of important events in our lives.

All of the examples mentioned above involve information from long-term, more or less permanent memory and they raise some intriguing questions for memory theory. For example, what kinds of information about common objects and events are stored in long-term memory and how can we reconcile such anecdotal evidence about real-life memory with theories of memory derived from laboratory studies?

An interesting example of research into real-life, long-term memory was provided by Nickerson and Adams's (1979) investigation of memory for a very common object, namely a penny. In separate experiments they used no less than five memory measures, to allow every chance of finding evidence that the details of the penny were well remembered. The memory measures included (a) drawing the coin, (b) drawing the coin given a list of features, (c) recognising features from a list, (d) indicating errors on an incorrectly drawn coin, and (e) recognising the correct drawing of the coin from among fifteen drawings. Subjects' performance was consistently poor on these tasks, often to their surprise and embarrassment. Even when subjects realised that a drawing was incorrect, they were generally not very accurate at identifying the errors. Indeed subjects not infrequently claimed that some correctly depicted features were in error.

In discussing their results Nickerson and Adams pointed out that we are not yet able to say precisely why memory is so poor for such a commonly encountered object as a penny. Nor were they able to specify exactly what attributes of a coin are stored in memory. The main workshop will be based on the experiments reported by Nickerson and Adams. Its aim will be to investigate aspects of memory for one or more commonly encountered everyday objects.

General procedure

First you will need to decide what common object(s) you will ask people to remember. You could use coins, as Nickerson and Adams did, or you could use paper currency, or think of some altogether different objects. For example, you might use telephone booths, bus tickets, post boxes, or fire hydrants. You will then have to decide what aspects of the to-be-remembered objects you will investigate. Following Nickerson and Adams, you could ask people to remember the form, or perhaps you could investigate size, weight, or colour of the object chosen. Nickerson and Adams did suggest that, for coins, colour and size might be better remembered than form because these are most important in discriminating among coins.

Nickerson and Adams used recall, recognition and reconstruction tasks to measure memory. Depending on which you feel are the most appropriate tasks, you could use any two or three of their tasks or some other task of your own devising. The tasks you choose should be relevant to the common object you are investigating and should also reflect your testing resources. Nevertheless, it would be interesting to compare at least two memory tests.

As Nickerson and Adams argued, recognition may be the most relevant test for coin memory since we normally need to recognise coins but rarely to recall their appearance. If you decide to use a recognition task with coins, then following their Experiment 5 would allow you to check on which global configurations of features are most likely to be regarded as correct. However, producing reasonably accurate and consistent representations of coins, and plausible distractors for recognition tests, will not be easy if you do not draw well. You could try photographic techniques, or you could try tracing the outlines or taking rubbings of the important features. Making these representations on tracing paper and overlaying them on a photocopier or using a cut-and-paste approach should allow you to produce quite good representations of 'rearranged' versions of the stimulus. Some banks may also be able to help you with drawings of currency.

If you are unable to arrange material for a recognition study, you could simply devise some questions about the design on your coins or other objects chosen, and have subjects recall the information. For example, on Australian currency, one coin features a platypus and one note depicts the history of flight. Can subjects correctly identify which these are?

You could either have quite a large number of subjects each making one response (cf. Nickerson and Adams's Experiment 4) or have fewer subjects each giving you more information as in the other experiments reported by Nickerson and Adams. Your choice here will depend on practical considerations as well as on your evaluation of the desirability of a repeated measures design. If you do decide to obtain a brief response from a large number of people, you could probably enlist some volunteers for a couple of minutes each, by simply approaching people on campus or in a local shopping centre.

For scoring your memory tests and for constructing recall cues or recognition tests you will need lists of actual and possible features of the objects you decide to investigate. Nickerson and Adams's Tables 1 and 2 should provide some useful hints here. Because coins and other common objects that you might test do change from time to time, you should keep in mind what features were on older versions when you are scoring. You could note any 'old' features subjects remember (cf. Nickerson and Adams, pp. 290-1).

For all the memory tests Nickerson and Adams used, and probably for those you will use, the most interesting analyses are the graphical treatments of different types of errors made (cf. Nickerson and Adams, Figures 2 and 3, and Table 3). Your data analysis will be largely descriptive, with a consideration of the number of completely correct responses and a classification of the various types of errors made.

Were your subjects as bad at remembering common objects as were Nickerson and Adams's subjects? You should consider whether any features and/or locations were better remembered than others. Why do you think people's long-term memory for such common objects is as deficient as Nickerson and Adams found? Although fascinating, such research into everyday memory tends not to be presented in the context of a detailed memory theory. Perhaps this is simply because work in this area is still quite new. How do you see such research fitting into memory theory? You could consider here Nickerson and Adams's emphasis on the usual uses of our memory for common objects. You might also discuss Nickerson and Adams's proposition (pp. 304 f) that it is difficult to distinguish what is actually remembered from what is inferred by subjects at the time of recall.

Alternatives

Although the Nickerson and Adams's study demonstrated that we have surprisingly poor memories for some common, frequently encountered objects, Brown and Kulik (1977) found that we *can* remember, with equally surprising and vivid detail, just what we were doing when we heard some particularly shattering piece of news many years ago (e.g. the assassination of President Kennedy). Brown and Kulik called such memories 'flashbulb memories' because the important news seemed to illuminate and maintain in memory many quite trivial details of the circumstances of hearing the news. In a questionnaire study, they found that most people had some flashbulb memories, although events which might trigger a 'flash' are likely to vary from person to person. They asked their subjects to rate the 'consequentiality' (importance to them) of the news which had triggered the flash, and also to indicate how often they had rehearsed the events surrounding their hearing the news. Such rehearsals typically involve relating the events to other people or listening to other accounts of the event. Brown and Kulik concluded that events which are very surprising and very consequential tend to elicit more rehearsal and to be remembered in more detail.

If you decide to follow up this research, then some fairly careful interviewing will be needed to encourage your subjects to recall the moment at which they were surprised or shocked by some (to them) important event. You could see whether these events have anything in common across subjects, and could investigate the extent to which they acted as a flashbulb to illuminate other more or less trivial aspects of the situation. You should also consider what other circumstantial facts your subjects cannot remember (e.g. the weather or clothing). If you were to use political events (e.g. in Australia the sacking of Prime Minister Gough Whitlam in 1975), then you could also obtain subjects' political affiliations which might to some extent parallel Brown and Kulik's racial membership variable. What mechanisms do you think lead to flashbulb memories and what implications do flashbulb memories have for memory theory?

A rather different approach to the sudy of long-term memory was provided by Rubin (1977), who asked American college students to recall culturally well-learned passages such as the Gettysburg Address, Hamlet's soliloquy, and the Twenty-third Psalm. On average his subjects had not encountered these passages for about three years. Contrary to much other research into discourse memory, Rubin found that subjects did not seem to remember just the gist of the passages: in fact they either remembered the exact wording or did not remember the passage at all. Moreover, subjects seemed to remember the passages in phrase units separated by breath pauses. As Rubin pointed out, this rote, associative long-term memory is contrary to many theories of long-term memory which stress semantic variables. Such theories would expect memory for gist but not exact surface form and surface features such as exact phrasing. You could investigate such long-term memory for prose or verse by using passages relevant to your culture. You might also consider whether it is likely that we use such long-term rote memory to remember things like telephone numbers, addresses, and car registration numbers. How could you test this? Keep in mind that a relatively large number of subjects may be required for this alternative since, as Rubin found, many people may be able to recall very little of any passage. What sorts of retrieval strategies do subjects use to recall this material?

Reference

Nickerson, R. S. and Adams, M. J. Long-term memory for a common object. *Cognitive Psychology*, 1979, **11**, 287–307.

References for Alternatives

Brown, R., and Kulik, J. Flashbulb memories. *Cognition*, 1977, 5, 73–99.
Rubin, D. C. Very long-term memory for prose and verse. *Journal of Verbal Learning and Behavior*, 1977, 16, 611–21.

III

Imagery

Introduction

Mental imagery has traditionally played a central role in psychologists' accounts of cognitive processes and in the representation of knowledge. It is an area, however, which is no stranger to controversy. Richardson (1969) outlined some of the past debates which have taken place on this topic. The main difficulty resides in providing an acceptable definition of the term *mental image*. It is a term that has proved difficult to operationalise, with many researchers using the term in idiosyncratic ways.

Currently, the major issue is whether visual imagery, in particular, should be used as an explanatory construct in psychology. Pylyshyn (1973) for example, has argued that the picture metaphor of imagery is misleading in that it suggests that information is stored as pictures in the head. He suggested instead, that our knowledge is stored in the form of abstract propositions. Kosslyn and Pomerantz (1977), on the other hand, suggested that imagery is a useful construct, arguing that images have properties that cannot be derived directly from more abstract propositional structures of the sort suggested by Pylyshyn. More recently, Anderson (1978) has argued that this is a semantic issue which cannot be decided empirically. Slightly different perspectives on this debate are contained in papers by Kieras (1978) and Wilton (1978).

The general term *mental imagery* has been used above, but current research has centered almost exclusively on visual imagery (an emphasis which is reflected in the workshops associated with this section). The focus within this area has changed in the last few years. Previously, research emphasised almost exclusively the mnemonic effectiveness of visual imagery. However, more recently, a growing body of research has emphasised the structure of imagery. The first approach is represented in the work of Paivio (1971), who presented overwhelming evidence that imagery provides an effective mnemonic code. For example, of two groups of subjects asked to remember a list of words, those instructed to form images of the words will recall more than those given no such instruction. Recently, researchers have started to ask questions about the nature and the structure of the visual image: for example, how does an image act as a repository of information? How does an image differ from a percept?

Both approaches are covered in the workshops. The books by Paivio (1971), Richardson (1969), and Sheehan (1972), provide a historical perspective, with examples illustrating the mnemonic approach to visual imagery mentioned above. Information on the second approach is contained mainly in research papers. Good summaries can be found in Finke (1980), Kosslyn and Pomerantz (1977), and Shepard (1978).

The seven workshops in this section can be divided into two categories. Two workshops (I1 and I2) are concerned with the use of imagery as an aid to remembering. The next four workshops (I3, I4, I5 and I6) examine the nature of the structure of visual imagery. The last workshop, (I7), spans both of these categories by examining how we represent the spatial environment in our minds.

Workshop I1 compares the mnemonic effectiveness of two methods of imagery — the method of loci and the peg-word system. The method of loci has been used since ancient Greek times as a memory aid. Workshop I2 asks whether bizarre images are remembered better than natural images. Despite the intuitive appeal of the claim that bizarre images are remembered better, results do not always support this.

The next four workshops are concerned with the nature of imagery. Workshop I3 is based on the work of Brooks (1968) and asks: how separate is our processing of visual and verbal material? Brooks's work marked a clear point in the changing interests of imagery researchers. He showed that imaging and perceiving in the same modality interfere with each other more than when two distinct modalities are involved. Workshop I4 asks whether imagining is like perceiving. It examines the memorial consequences of information that is seen and information that is imagined. Workshop I5 is concerned with the spatial structure of the visual image. It examines the work of Kosslyn (1975), who argued that since it is hard to discriminate details of small stimuli in perception, we might find it similarly hard to discriminate details of relatively small images. Workshop I6 investigates whether we can turn images in our head. It is based on recent work which suggests that we can and do rotate images mentally in order to make comparisons. Workshop I7 asks whether we store accurate representations of the world in which we live (e.g. our local suburb). It is based on work which has suggested that we retain an idealised version of our environment rather that an accurate representation.

The concept of mental imagery is very much a part of our mental activity. The area is currently enjoying such a revival that a new periodical was published in mid-1977 entitled the *Journal of Mental Imagery*.

References

Anderson, J. R. Arguments concerning representation for mental imagery. *Psychological Review*, 1978, **85**, 249-77.

Brooks, L. R. Spatial and verbal components of the act of recall. *Canadian Journal of Psychology*, 1968, **22**, 349–68.

Finke, R. A. Levels of equivalence in imagery and perception. *Psychological Review*, 1980, **87**, 113–32.

Kieras, D. Beyond pictures and words: Alternative information-processing models for imagery effects in verbal memory. *Psychological Bulletin*, 1978, **85**, 532–54.

Kosslyn, S. M. Information represented in visual images. *Cognitive Psychology*, 1975, **7**, 341–70.

Kosslyn, S. M., and Pomerantz, J. R. Imagery, propositions, and the form of internal representations. *Cognitive Psychology*, 1977, **9**, 52–76.

Paivio, A. *Imagery and Verbal Processes*. New York: Holt, Rinehart & Winston, 1971.

Pylyshyn, Z. W. What the mind's eye tells the mind's brain: A critique of mental imagery. *Psychological Bulletin*, 1973, **80**, 1–24.

Richardson, A. *Mental Imagery*. London: Routledge & Kegan Paul, 1969.

Sheehan, P. W. (ed.). *The Function and Nature of Imagery*. London: Academic Press, 1972.

Shepard, R. N. The mental image. *American Psychologist*, 1978, **33**, 125–37.

Wilton, R. M. Explaining imaginal inference by operations in a propositional format. *Perception*, 1978, **7**, 563–74.

11 The method of loci

A walk down memory lane?

We shall imagine the man in question as lying ill in bed, if we know him personally. If we do not know him, we shall yet take someone to be our invalid, but not a man of the lowest class, so that he may come to mind at once. And we shall place the defendant at the bedside, holding in his right hand a cup, in his left, tablets, and on the fourth finger, a ram's testicles. In this way we can have in memory the man who was poisoned, the witness, and the inheritance. (cited in F. Yates, *The Art of Memory*, 1966, p. 11)

Since time immemorial man has been interested in a variety of techniques for improving his ability to remember. One method, called the 'method of loci' has been known since the time of Cicero. The method involves an individual imagining a set of locations (loci) along a familiar route. Each of these locations can be linked to an item to be remembered. When the time comes to recall the memory items, the individual simply imagines walking along the route and retrieving the memory item from the locations.

A study by Ross and Lawrence (1968) attests to the utility of the method of loci. They asked their subjects to familiarise themselves with a sequence of locations (the loci) around a university campus. After familiarisation was completed, the rationale behind the method of loci was explained to the subjects. Subjects were then presented, on successive days, with lists of forty words and instructed to use the method of loci to remember the words. After they had mentally placed the words at loci along their imagined walk, subjects were asked to recall as many as they could. They were also tested for recall on the subsequent day and then were presented with a new list of forty words. Recall immediately after using the method of loci for remembering the words averaged thirty-eight out of forty in correct serial order; a day later recall averaged thirty-four out of the forty items in correct order. These results are markedly superior to the recall expected for subjects who simply try to remember the words as a list (Ross and Lawrence did not actually include this comparison control group).

Little is understood about why the method of loci is a powerful memory device. Bower (1970) for example, suggests that the use of actual geographical locations is not crucial for the mnemonic effect. He points out that equally good recall can be produced by the 'numeric pegword' system. This system is similar to the method of loci except an extra stage of learning is necessary. It initially requires the over-learning of associations between a sequence of numbers and a sequence of concrete objects which also rhyme with the numbers; e.g. 'one is a sun', 'two is glue', 'three is a flea', and so on. When recall is required the pegword system is used in exactly the same way as the method of loci with memory items being imagined with the pegwords instead of the loci.

This workshop tests Bower's claim that the two methods produce equal results. Bower does not produce evidence to support his claim and there seems reason to doubt its validity. It appears possible that more confusion would occur using the pegword system with a long list of items than using the method of loci. This assertion is based on the potential confusability of numbers. Up to the number twenty the numbers are discrete in sound and are unlikely to be confused. But then some sound repetition occurs — Twenty-one, Thirty-one, Forty-one, and so on. The number one in each case introduces a possible confusion element with the associated rhyme. A subject may think 'Twenty-one bun or was it sun?'

General procedure

You will be testing memory for words under three independent conditions: (i) using intentional memory instructions (Group 1, the control group), (ii) using the method of loci as a mnemonic aid (Group 2), (iii) using the pegword system (Group 3). You will need to give Group 2 and 3 subjects appropriate instructions on the use of their mnemonic device in addition to allowing them sufficient time to learn their system. You should test subjects' learning of their mnemonic technique prior to presenting the word lists and if necessary allow extra time for the device to be learnt properly. A comparison of the effectiveness of the two systems assumes that both are equally well learnt.

When subjects are ready, read your list of memory words (concrete nouns are preferable for this purpose). Given the rationale of this workshop, the longer the lists the better — approximately fifty words per list should be sufficient. It is up to you how many lists you present: additional lists may throw some light on the differential effectiveness of the two mnemonic systems across lists and of practice effects for mnemonic devices. As in the Ross and Lawrence experiment, the subjects' task is to free-recall as many of the listed words as possible after each list has been presented. However, you may find as they did, that subjects will recall the items in serial order, especially in the two mnemonic conditions.

Analysis of the data would involve a comparison of the mean correct words recalled per condition across the trials. A fuller analysis of the data could involve a two-way analysis of variance with repeated measures on the trials factor. Subsidiary analysis might involve looking at the nature of errors — especially in the two mnemonic conditions.

Do you think the comparison between the two mnemonic systems is reasonable? Even if Bower's claims are substantiated and performances were equal under the two mnemonic systems, does this imply that the use of geographical locations in the method of loci is unnecessary? What everyday uses can you think of for either of the two methods? We have dealt with single, isolated words in this experiment: do you think the approach could be extended to include more complex meaningful material, e.g. objects or pictures? You could also discuss what other mnemonic techniques are available. In his article, Bower carefully analyses the various components of the method of loci, so it may be worth discussing the validity of Bower's analysis.

Alternatives

You could change and extend the experiment outlined above in a number of ways. For example, the retention interval between presentation of the word lists and recall could be systematically altered, as could the list lengths themselves. The latter may be an important manipulation if the confusion argument outlined at the end of the introduction has any validity. The types of words used in the lists could also be varied. For example, you may get an interaction effect between the nature of the words (e.g. noun/adjective: concrete/abstract words) and the type of mnemonic device used. This suggests that perhaps different mnemonic systems suit different task requirements and materials.

Winograd and Lynn (1979) suggest that the facilitative effect of imagery on recall is related to two factors; (i) the interactive nature of the image, and (ii) the uniqueness of the imagined context (i.e. the imagined setting in which an image is placed). They argue that the potential role of redundancy or uniqueness of the imagined context has been ignored by studies comparing interactive and separation imagery. An interactive image is one in which two items are imaged in interaction with one another, whereas separation imagery involves an image of two separate non-interacting items. Winograd and Lynn found that interactive imagery is little affected by context uniqueness whereas separation imagery is. You could repeat Winograd and Lynn's experiment or you could examine their claims using the two mnemonic techniques discussed above. For example, you could examine their claim that interactive imagery is little affected by context by comparing performance on a list of words when few loci or pegwords are used (i.e. multiple use of each locus) with performance when the loci or pegwords are used only once. You might consider whether Winograd and Lynn's model applies to the two mnemonic devices discussed here.

References

Bower, G. H. Analysis of a mnemonic device. *American Scientist*, 1970, **58**, 496–510.

Ross, J., and Lawrence, K. A. Some observations on a memory artifice. *Psychonomic Science*, 1968, **13**, 107–8.

Yates, F. A. *The Art of Memory*, London: Routledge and Kegan Paul, 1966.

Reference for Alternatives

Winograd, E., and Lynn, D. S. Role of contextual imagery in associative recall. *Memory & Cognition*, 1979, **7**, 29–34.

12 Bizarre imagery as a mnemonic device

Does bizarre imagery facilitate remembering?

For centuries professional mnemonists have claimed that memory will be facilitated most by making the mediating memory image as bizarre as possible. Despite the intuitive appeal of this claim, it has not received strong support in recent research. For example, Nappe and Wollen (1973) found in a paired-associate learning task, using word pairs, that instruction to form bizarre images produced no more correct responses on recall than did instructions to form natural images. On the other hand, Andreoff and Yarmey (1976), in a similar experimental set-up, found that bizarre imagery did facilitate recall.

One possible reason for the two different sets of results may lie in the nature of instructions given to the subjects. Nappe and Wollen's subjects were not told that their memory would be tested: that is, an incidental memory technique was used. Subjects thought the experimenters were interested primarily in studying the time it took to produce either bizarre or natural images. In the Andreoff and Yarmey experiment, however, subjects were aware that they would be required to recall the word pairs. Perhaps it is the incidental task used by Nappe and Wollen which prevented finding an effect in favour of bizarre imagery.

However, there is a second problem which may have affected results. Subjects were required to change the type of imagery they used from trial to trial in both experiments mentioned above. If subjects are required on one trial to use bizarre imagery and on the next natural imagery, the experimenter probably has little control over what the subject is actually doing on any one trial. To avoid this possible problem it seems important that experiments in this area use an independent groups design — with one group performing exclusively under bizarre imagery instructions, and a second group performing exclusively under natural imagery instructions. Bizarre and natural imagery may have different effects on the memory under different types of experimental instructions (i.e. intentional or incidental memory instructions) and using different experimental designs (i.e. a mixed group or an independent groups design).

This workshop is based on the two experiments discussed above. It will examine the different effects on memory of bizarre and natural imagery using an independent groups design with incidental memory instructions.

General procedure

You will need to construct a list of paired-associates (see Paivio, Yuille and Madigan, 1968, for word norms). An overhead projector would be an efficient means of presenting your word pairs: otherwise you could read out the word pairs. Nappe and Wollen point out that earlier experimenters may not have found an effect because too few word pairs were used to obtain a substantial difference between the two types of imagery instructions. About forty word pairs would seem sufficient to overcome this problem.

As the basic design is an independent groups design, you need to give your subjects separate experimental instructions. So that you can run both groups together it is suggested that you have two separate sets of instruction sheets (one containing bizarre imagery instructions, the other containing natural imagery instructions). Because we are investigating the effect of incidental memory instructions, the subjects must not become aware that there will be a memory test. Therefore you have to word your instruction sheet in a plausible way. For example, both groups can be asked to rate on a five-point scale the ease with which the word pairs form an interacting visual image. Prior to the commencement of the task the natural imagery group could be given to illustrative examples of ordinary interactions to guide their ratings (e.g. DOG and BALL), while the bizarre imagery group could be given examples of unrelated words to guide their ratings (e.g. DOG and CIGAR). The instruction sheet should contain not only the instructions but also space to make judgments for the forty word pairs on a one- to five-point rating scale. It is suggested you allow 10 seconds per word pair for subjects to make their decisions. After you have presented the forty word pairs, collect subjects' rating sheets. Allow an interval of several minutes before informing the group that a memory test will follow. In this phase of the experiment you present one word of the word pair and ask subjects to write down the missing associated word. It is a good idea to randomise presentation of the words in the test phase to overcome order effects.

Analysis of the data involves calculating the mean number of words correctly recalled for the two instruction groups. A simple *t*-test should suffice for statistical analysis. Does the bizarre imagery group recall more than the natural imagery group? You might also analyse the imagery rating scales. Do subjects indicate that bizarre images are easier to form than natural images? Is there any relationship between ease of forming an image and subsequent memory?

The term *bizarre imagery* has been used frequently in this workshop. In discussion, you might consider what would constitute an adequate definition of bizarre imagery. Andreoff and Yarmey (1976) point out that professional mnemonists consider the bizarre quality of imagery an important aid when material has to be remembered over an extended time period. They also point out that most experiments investigate bizarreness in immediate recall situations. You might discuss how bizarre imagery would operate over an extended time period.

Alternatives

Given Andreoff and Yarmey's point above concerning the likely effect of bizarre imagery over time, you could run the experiment comparing immediate with delayed recall. Webber and Marshall (1978) have found that bizarre imagery leads to better memory than natural imagery over a one-week interval, supporting Andreoff and Yarmey's contention. You could also retain the independent groups design but give subjects intentional instructions. You might also run the experiment with subjects receiving both sets of imagery instructions in addition to manipulating memory instructions. These experiments would address in a thorough way the problem whether or not memory instructions are the crucial factor affecting results. You could contrast highly concrete word pairs such as 'dog' and 'ball', with performance on abstract word pairs such as 'god' and 'love'. It is possible that instructions to form bizarre and natural images, respectively, may have differential effects on these differing types of word pairs.

A further alternative would be to use pictures rather than word pairs. Webber and Marshall (1978) presented pictures of two objects which were in either a bizarre or a natural interaction. Advantages of this procedure are that individual differences in the ability to construct images are minimised and control of bizarreness of the image is maintained. However, it could be claimed that such a procedure minimises the use of imagery, and subjects' performance may reflect visual memory ability rather than imagery ability. This issue could be investigated by conducting an experiment contrasting bizarre and natural imagery performance on picture pairs with performance on equivalent word pairs. Do your results support Webber and Marshall's contention that the facilitative effects of bizarre imagery are limited to longer retention intervals and situations involving deeper processing?

References

Andreoff, G. R., and Yarmey, A. D. Bizarre imagery and associative learning: A confirmation. *Perceptual and Motor Skills*, 1976, **43**, 143-8.

Nappe, G. W. and Wollen, K. A. Effects of instruction to form common and bizarre mental images on retention. *Journal of Experimental Psychology*, 1973, **100**, 6-8.

Paivio, A., Yuille, J. C., and Madigan, S. Concreteness, imagery and meaningfulness values for 925 nouns. *Journal of Experimental Psychology Monograph Supplement*, 1968, **76**, 1-25.

Reference for Alternatives

Webber, S. M., and Marshall, P. H. Bizarreness effects in imagery as a function of processing level and delay. *Journal of Mental Imagery*, 1978, **2**, 291-300.

13 The independence of visual and verbal codes

How separate is our processing of visual and verbal material?

> ... and now we enter the magical world of mental images ... step right up for bizarre wonderful sights. First Professor Brooks showing how the mind works its ways differently for verbal and spatial materials. Others will astound, compound and confound. Come enter the wonderful world of mentalism ... (Norman, 1976, p. 157)

If you have tried driving a car along a winding road while listening to a tennis match on the car-radio you will probably have experienced some conflict between the act of driving and the task of visualising the play. As Baddeley, Grant, Wight, and Thomson (1975) mentioned, you will probably experience less conflict if you listen to music instead. Anecdotal evidence of this kind suggests that if you try to imagine a spatial scene at the same time as carrying out spatial movements, the two activities will interfere with one another. Similar anecdotal evidence suggests verbal information from memory (auditory images) must at some point be in the same form as verbal information entering the sensory system — and thus interference is likely to occur. Brooks (1968) investigated the notion that verbal and spatial information are handled in distinct, modality-specific ways by obtaining data from experiments which induced a conflict between overt responding and the act of recall.

In one of Brooks's experiments subjects were asked to image a block figure of a capital F and to 'go around' the block figure mentally, responding at each corner 'yes' if it was either at the top or bottom of the figure, or 'no' if it was not. In three conditions subjects indicated their responses by (1) saying 'yes' or 'no', (2) tapping their left or right fingers, or (3) pointing to 'Y' or 'N' in a pattern of symbols. Subjects took longer time to respond when using a visual device to point out their answer (condition 3). Brooks was careful to eliminate the possibility that pointing to the visual Y or N was itself a more difficult response than the other two response formats, by a second condition in which subjects had to memorise a sentence (e.g. 'A bird in the hand is not in the bush'). Subjects were required to think through the sentence and classify each word as either a noun or not. In this situation the verbal response (saying 'yes' or 'no') took longer than the other two conditions. Taken together, these findings indicate that dealing with new visual information interferes with visual imagery, whereas verbal output interferes with auditory (verbal) imaging.

The main part of this workshop will replicate part of the Brooks's study.

General procedure

However you decide to approach this workshop it is a good idea to test Brooks's exact procedure on parents/friends first — it looks more complex from a first reading than it really is! When you have tried it out, you might then like to make some modifications to the stimuli or to the procedure. Whatever stimuli you use, make sure you have the same number of decisions to be made for visual as for auditory material.

If you adopt the procedure outlined by Brooks in his Experiment 1, use only two response methods, for example, pointing and speaking, with two types of material (visual and verbal). As in the Brooks experiment, subjects can perform both tasks. In addition, check whether or not subjects respond correctly to all the corners of the stimulus figures, as well as the time taken to complete the task. Brooks did not check for errors, i.e. number of corners responded to minus the correct number of corners. This seems an omission since it is possible the results obtained by Brooks are due to a time/error trade-off. That is, subjects responded faster in the low-conflict conditions, but made more errors.

Subjects will need to work in pairs, one performing the task, the other recording the two response measures (viz. time taken to complete the task and number of responses made). The students recording the responses will need a stopwatch to measure time taken for task completion. Make sure your subjects know what nouns and articles are — some don't! All stimulus materials can be presented to the group by the person running the workshop, or separately by the experimenter within each pair. After completing this testing, and with appropriately counterbalanced controls on the stimuli, subjects could switch roles, with the experimenter becoming the subject, and vice versa.

The basic design of this experiment is a 2×2 factorial with repeated measures on both factors (i.e. type of input material and type of response). It is probably best to base discussion on the mean response time in each cell. The high-conflict conditions in these experiments are likely to show a much higher variance than the low-conflict conditions, making detailed statistical analysis difficult.

In discussion, you might consider whether this experiment is analogous to the driving situation mentioned earlier. In what other ways could you examine the response conflict in the driving situation? Did your results show a time/error trade-off? If this did occur, how would it affect Brooks's interpretations? What does the kind of conflict experienced in this type of experiment tell us about the nature of mental representation? In the light of

Brooks's findings and discussions, you could also consider exactly what can be meant by 'modality specific processing'.

Alternatives

There are a number of alternatives to this workshop in Brooks's eight experiments in which he tries to establish the locus of effect. Any one of these experiments offers an alternative workshop.

A number of other workers have used Brooks's technique to examine analogous problems. For example, Baddeley *et al.* examined the interference between imagery and performance on a motor task, which is probably closer to the driving interference example than the experiments reported by Brooks. You could try their tracking task with concurrent visualisation, following their Experiments 1 and 2. Alternatively, you might take up their suggestion (p. 215) that it is active visualising which is disrupted by a visual task, by examining the effects of a task like visual tracking on using mnemonic techniques such as the pegword system.

Phillips and Christie (1977) have criticised the conclusion from Brooks's experiments that special-purpose visual processors are implicated in producing the interference effects. (In fact, Brooks himself is careful to use the term 'spatial' rather than visual throughout his paper, so the criticism applies more to those who later interpreted his findings in this way.) You could explore further the suggestion of Phillips and Christie that the nature of the interfering task needs to be analysed to see what are its important aspects. For example, using their recognition paradigm, you could make the visualisation required by the intervening task more active. In discussion, you could consider whether you prefer the capacity interference approach of Phillips and Christie or the structural interference approach of Brooks. What similarities can you trace between Phillips and Christie's conclusions on the important characteristics of interference and those reached by Baddeley *et al.*?

References

Brooks, L. R. Spatial and verbal components of the act of recall. *Canadian Journal of Psychology*, 1968, **22**, 349–68.
Baddeley, A. D. Grant, S., Wight, E., and Thomson, N. Imagery and visual working memory. In P. M. A. Rabbitt & S. Dornic (eds) *Attention and Performance* (vol. 5). London: Academic Press, 1975.

Reference for Alternatives

Phillips, W. A. and Christie, D. F. M. Interference with visualization. *Quarterly Journal of Experimental Psychology*, 1977, **29**, 637–50.

14 Imagery and perception
Is imagining like perceiving?

The experience of visual imagery seems to be quite common. Most of us claim we can see absent aspects of our environment (e.g. people, places and objects) in our 'mind's eye'. When we imagine seeing an object, the sensation seems to be visual in nature. Given this sensation, a reasonable question is: to what degree is visual imagery akin to visual perception and what is the overlap between the two processes? This workshop examines the question.

An experiment by Peterson and Graham (1974) suggested that subjects were faster at seeing an object in a stimulus array if they first imagined that object. They argued that this result supports the view that visual perception and visual imagery involve similar mechanisms. Peterson (1975) further explored the relationship between imagery and perception within a memory paradigm. He suggested that if imagery is dependent upon or arises from reconstruction of perceptions (i.e. involves similar mechanisms), the pattern of recall of material imagined should resemble the pattern of material actually seen.

Peterson tested this suggestion using recall of letters arranged in 4×4 matrices. There were three groups: the first saw the matrices, the second were told their contents. The third group, like the second, were told the letters, but with the added instruction to form an image of the matrix as it was described. Those who saw the matrices performed best. The group who heard them described, and formed images, were superior to the group who were instructed merely to listen. Moreover, the pattern of individual cell recall for the 'imagery' and the 'seen' groups was similar, with the corner cells of the matrix being recalled best in both conditions. No such pattern emerged in the verbal description group. Peterson argues that this result indicates that both seen and imaged matrices were stored in similar spatial formats, resulting in similar recall patterns. These results also support the view that visual perception and visual imagery involve similar mechanisms.

This workshop will be based on a partial replication of Peterson's study examining the relationship between memory for seen and imaged information.

General procedure

You could follow the approach outlined by Peterson, with some differences. Use only a 3 X 3 matrix, not a 4 X 4 matrix, as our experience suggests that Peterson's subjects may have been exceptionally talented to cope with a 4 X 4 matrix. Because the main interest of this workshop lies in a comparison between the 'imagined' and the 'seen' conditions, it is suggested that you examine only these two conditions, leaving out the verbal condition. Also, unless you have time to spare or unless more than one person is involved as an experimenter in this workshop, you could use a repeated measures design, with all subjects performing under the imagined and the seen conditions. This may introduce some confounding of effects, but it saves on materials and time. However, you will have to randomise presentation of the imagined and the seen trials.

The materials needed for this workshop are an overhead projector for presenting the seen matrices and a tape recorder for presenting the information contained in the cells of the imagined matrices. If a tape recorder is not available, you can present the information for the imagery group verbally. You will also need to construct test booklets to measure your subjects' recall. It is suggested that you follow the probe-recall technique used by Peterson in which subjects are shown a matrix with three cells signalled for recall. Subjects do not know from trial to trial which three cells will be left empty. They simply have to recall the information contained in these cells. The aim of this technique is to prevent subjects from selecting a particular part of the matrix for special attention rather than trying to remember it all.

Design your experiment keeping in mind the amount of time you have available. If you sample each cell of the matrix three times (the minimum number of observations for useful data) for both seen and imagined conditions, and on each trial you test memory for three cells, then you will need a total of eighteen trials. Each trial, composed of presentation of material, followed by a short interval, followed by the probe-recall test, takes about one minute; thus on the above calculation you should allow approximately twenty minutes for collection of the data.

Analysis of the data involves working out the proportion of correct items recalled for each individual cell of the 3 X 3 matrices, across all subjects, for both imagined and seen conditions. You can then compare your pattern of results with those of Peterson. A more detailed analysis, comparing the individual cells, can be carried out using multiple Tukey tests.

In discussing the results you could consider whether the repeated measures design introduces too many confounding variables. You could also discuss whether this experiment really examines the spatial nature of a visual image. In what other ways could we investigate the spatial nature of the image?

Alternatives

Retaining the recall technique outlined above, you could change the nature of the material used in the matrix. Instead of using letters as Peterson did, you could, for example, use common objects. Further you could test the spatial memory for an array of objects which might normally occur in some kind of spatial relationship (e.g. dog, bone) as against an array which is unrelated (e.g. plane, carrot).

A recognition technique might be considered more appropriate to test for spatial properties. It is possible to re-run the experiment outlined above using a recognition technique. Instead of testing each individual matrix directly after presentation (either seen or imagined), you present your matrices one after another and then test, using a recognition paradigm in which subjects have to pick out the matrices which they originally saw or imaged from a set of distractors. This would allow you to examine the relationship between imagery and perceiving in a different way.

Peterson, Peterson, and Ward-Hull (1977) examined the effect of rehearsal opportunities and interfering activities upon the retention of images. A similar methodology was used to the one described above, except that subjects were presented with numbers instead of letters and two successive matrices rather than just one. They had to recall only the first matrix, only the second matrix, both matrices, or the sum of the matrices. Subjects were told prior to, or subsequent to the matrices' presentation what recall would be required. It would be interesting to compare recall performance of constructed image matrices with seen matrices using the experimental manipulations of Peterson *et al.* (1977). If Peterson (1975) is correct and imagery is dependent upon or arises from reconstruction of perceptions (i.e. the two processes involve similar mechanisms), then the pattern of results in the imagery condition and the seen condition should be similar given the same experimental manipulations.

References

Peterson, M. J., Graham, S. E. Visual detection and visual imagery. *Journal of Experimental Psychology*, 1974, **103**, 509–14.

Peterson, M. J. The retention of imagined and seen spatial matrices. *Cognitive Psychology*, 1975, **7**, 181–93.

Reference for Alternatives

Peterson, M. J., Peterson, L. A., and Ward-Hull, C. Rehearsing and retaining mental matrices. *Journal of Verbal Learning and Verbal Behavior*, 1977, **16**, 371–81.

15 The structure of imagery
How good is your image?

The nature of the visual image has long been debated both within and outside psychology. Recent research suggests that we process and react to visual images much as we do to percepts. Kosslyn in a number of studies (e.g. Kosslyn, 1975) has attempted to demonstrate the commonality of visual imagery and visual perception. Although his experiments do not directly compare imaging and perceiving, he does argue that his experiments indicate that making a decision about the properties of visual images can be equated with making decisions about the properties of percepts.

Kosslyn (1975) points out that in perception parts of visual stimuli are more difficult to resolve when the stimuli are small than when they are large. From this observation he hypothesises that it would be more difficult to say whether an imaged object has a specified property when the image is small than when the image is large. Kosslyn asked subjects to judge whether or not a certain property (e.g. has claws) was appropriate for an animal they had been asked to image. For example, a subject might hear 'cat', followed some seconds later by 'claws'. The subject is to construct an image of a cat upon hearing its name, and then inspect this image for claws, indicating whether or not claws are a property of the imaged cat. Although Kosslyn's basic experimental measures were reaction times (RTs), he was not interested merely in how quickly a property's appropriateness could be judged, but rather in how quickly a person could utilise an image to determine whether or not a property belonged to a given animal. To test the hypothesis that it would be more difficult to confirm a property as appropriate when the image is small, Kosslyn manipulated image size. Every animal which was to be judged was imaged adjacent to either an imaged elephant or a fly. This manipulation was based on the assumption that the greater the area of an adjacent image, the smaller the image in the remaining 'space' and therefore the more time required to make a judgment about it.

This workshop is based on the work of Kosslyn (1975, Experiment 1) and tests the hypothesis that it takes longer to make decisions about images if they are small than if they are large. Do we treat images like percepts?

General procedure

For this workshop you will need a number of timing devices – chronoscopes would be ideal. You will need a list of animals and a list of properties. Remember that on half the trials the properties should be able to be judged as inappropriate. Twenty test trials should be sufficient. In addition you will need to prepare some practice trials to familiarise subjects with the task. Students can work in pairs, one acting as the subject making the appropriate judgments, the other as the experimenter recording the RTs associated with the judgments. The sequence of events for each judgment would be as follows: (a) the student running the workshop reads out either 'elephant' or 'fly' followed by the name of an animal (e.g. 'cat'), followed by a property (e.g. 'claw'); (b) when they hear the name of the property, the experimenters start the chronoscopes; (c) the subject depresses the switch as he/she responds either 'Yes' or 'No'; (d) the experimenter records the subject's time and decision. As mentioned above it is important to stress that subjects actually examine their image carefully in making their judgments.

The basic design is a 2 × 2 factorial with repeated measures on both factors: size of initial image (small or large) × appropriateness of property (yes or no).

Do you think that Kosslyn's experiments and yours demonstrate that making judgments about the properties of images is not dissimilar to making judgments about percepts? A rather crucial discussion question is whether you think you need to invoke the concept of imagery to explain these findings. You could ask your subjects how they completed the task. In what other ways could you test for similarities between the image and the percept? Can you think of a more direct test than the approach taken by Kosslyn?

Alternatives

There are a number of alternatives to the experiments outlined above to be found in the 1975 paper. In another paper, Kosslyn (1973) approached the problem by using a memory-imagery paradigm. He showed his subjects drawings, each consisting of an outline object with three small objects contained within it, arranged either horizontally or vertically (e.g. a tower with a flag at the top, a window half-way down, and a door at the bottom). Some subjects were later instructed to recall each picture as a visual image while focussing on the contained object at one end (top/bottom, e.g. the flag or the door). They were then asked to judge whether a named object was depicted in the picture. Kosslyn found that it took the shortest time to verify the presence of a focussed item and the longest time to verify the presence of an item at the opposite end of the imaged picture. These results were interpreted as demonstrating that the time taken to scan for objects at various locations on an image is a function of their distance from a focus point.

These results, however, are open to a different interpretation. In mentally scanning the image from one end to the other more elements may be passed over than when scanning from the middle of an image to one of its ends. The results may be a function of the difference in time taken mentally to examine either adjacent or non-adjacent items in a memory list rather than a function of the time taken to cover some distance on a visual image. In an attempt to resolve this issue Kosslyn, Ball and Reiser (1978) asked subjects to memorise a map of an island containing seven landmarks. Subjects' response latencies were measured for the times taken to scan betwen landmarks. The results supported the imagery hypothesis by showing that response latencies were related to the physical distance between landmarks and not to the number of intervening items.

However, Kosslyn *et al.*'s interpretation has recently been questioned by Mitchell and Richman (1980), who demonstrated that experimental demand characteristics may be operating in the image-scanning studies. They argued that this factor must be controlled before we can assume that response latencies are a function of image scanning. What do you think of these criticisms? You could replicate their experimental manipulations on any of the Kosslyn tasks cited above. It would be a test of your ingenuity to design an experiment which controls experimental demand characteristics and tests the hypothesis that there is a positive relationship between image scanning distance and reaction time.

References

Kosslyn, S. M. Information represented in visual images. *Cognitive Psychology*. 1975, 7, 341–70.

References for Alternatives

Kosslyn, S. M. Scanning visual images: Some structural implications. *Perception & Psychophysics*, 1973, 14, 90–4.

Kosslyn, S. M., Ball, T. M., and Reiser, B. J. Visual images preserve metric spatial information: Evidence from studies of image scanning. *Journal of Experimental Psychology: Human Perception and Performance*, 1978, 4, 47–60.

Mitchell, D. B., and Richman, C. L. Confirmed reservations: Mental travel. *Journal of Experimental Psychology: Human Perception and Performance*, 1980, 6, 58–66.

16 Mental rotation
Can we turn images in our head?

People who try to find their way around an unfamiliar city by using a map engage at some stage in mental rotation. They have probably turned part of the map in their head to get a better 'view' of it. Similar problems requiring mental rotation are assembling the pieces of a jigsaw puzzle or rearranging the furniture layout of a room in your head. How do we perform these activities? Do we have to use visual imagery to perform the task? Is the mental activity involved analogous to actually watching something rotate? Cooper and Shepard (1978, especially pp. 111–35) reported a number of experiments designed to establish the nature of rotation and other imagery transformations. In particular they were interested in the similarity between mental rotation and perceiving something rotate.

The main technique they used involved subjects making judgments of whether a stimulus (e.g., a capital letter R) was presented normally or as a mirror image. They found that the further the stimulus was rotated from the upright, the longer the subject took to make this judgment. It has therefore been suggested that subjects have mentally to rotate the image to the upright before they can make a decision. The general finding is that the time/angle function is always monotonic, often remarkably linear, for a variety of stimuli. Subjects evidently rotate each character mentally to the upright in order to match it with some internal representation of the standard version of the character.

This workshop is based on the comparison of two slightly different approaches used by Cooper and Shepard. The first involved subjects' matching a rotated test stimulus (0°, 60°, 120°, 180°, 240°, 300° from the upright) with a standard non-reversed upright version presented simultaneously, and indicating whether the test stimulus was the same as the standard figure or a reversed version. The second approach was similar, except that the comparison standard character was omitted and subjects had to say whether the test stimulus was normal or reversed (e.g. a normal or mirror-image alphabetical letter). Subjects in these tasks had to make this decision as rapidly as they could without making errors. Cooper and Shepard (p. 134) suggested that these approaches would lead to slightly different strategies and results, with reaction time and rotation speed being slower when the standard is simultaneously presented with the test stimulus.

General procedure

It is suggested that, for ease of running the workshop, you concentrate on one stimulus (e.g. the capital letter *R*). Accurate timing of subjects' responses is crucial in this study. Therefore you will need either a tachistoscope or a slide projector which has a light-sensitive cell attached to the lens, which, when activated, could start a series of timing devices such as chronoscopes. The advantage of using a projector is that subjects can be tested in groups.

You need to construct two sets of stimuli: the first set with a test figure and a comparison figure on the same card or slide (Set 1), the second with a single test figure (Set 2). Both sets of stimuli contain twelve individual stimulus cards — one normal and one reversed at each of six orientations. This means you need to construct twenty-four individual stimuli in all. In addition you will need to construct some practice items to familiarise subjects with the task. To maximise the data obtained in the workshop it is a good idea to test all subjects with both Sets 1 and 2, simply randomising the order of presenting the sets. Presentation order of stimulus orientations should also be randomised. Probably four observations per orientation per subject would be sufficient.

If time is severely limited, our experience suggests that one observation per orientation per subject will do if the final analysis is on medians rather than means for each orientation. In addition, given the symmetry of reaction times around 180° that Cooper and Shepard reported (p. 117), you could perhaps just test four orientations rather than all six. With sufficient time you might repeat trials on which the subject makes an error since only correct reaction times will be analysed. You could also include a final questionnaire asking subjects how they thought they had performed the task.

In analysis of the data you will need to calculate each subject's median reaction times for correct responses at each orientation, for both the normal and reversed letters, and for Set 1 and Set 2. You can then graph means of these subject medians, on the ordinate, against degrees of orientation on the abscissa. You might also check whether there were any systematic effects on the number of errors.

In discussion you should consider any differences which emerged between Sets 1 and 2. Did your reaction times increase linearly with angle of orientation? You might also consider the strategies your subjects reported using and whether they seemed to execute rotations smoothly or in discrete steps. You could consider whether there was much variation in rotation speed among your subjects. What do your results and those of previous researchers suggest about the nature of and the use of imagery? In what other ways could we perform the mental rotation tasks?

Alternatives

There are a number of alternatives to the present experiment contained in Cooper and Shepard's paper. For example, you could use drawings of three-dimensional shapes, or random shapes, instead of letters. Alternatively you could investigate some of the spatial transformations, other than rotation, which Cooper and Shepard mentioned.

A new twist on mental rotation was provided by Carpenter and Eisenberg's (1978) demonstration of mental rotation by congenitally blind and blindfolded sighted subjects in a haptic variant of Cooper and Shepard's task. This suggests that mental rotation need not be visual. Without necessarily using blind subjects you could use a haptic rotation task to see whether you also obtain the monotonic increase in reaction time with increasing angular displacement which suggests mental rotation. With more difficulty you might even be able to devise variants of the rotation task in other modalities.

Pylyshyn (1979) offered both theoretical arguments and experimental evidence to support his criticism of a 'holistic analogue' view of mental rotation. Although his definition of analogical imagery processing is not precisely the same as Cooper and Shepard's, his arguments are well worth pursuing and you could follow up or extend his experimental evidence.

Alternatively you might follow Pinker and Finke (1980) who used a fairly complex three-dimensional rotation task to investigate the properties of images and the processes of rotation in more detail. With sufficient time for lengthy individual testing and possibly with two experimenters you might follow up this study. In particular you could try asking subjects to rotate other sorts of three-dimensional objects, for example, a model of the solar system or perhaps a model including several buildings of your university or college.

Reference

Cooper, L. A., and Shepard, R. N. Transformations on representations of objects in space. In E. C. Carterette & M. P. Friedman (eds). *Handbook of Perception* (vol. 8): *Perceptual Coding.* New York: Academic Press, 1978.

References for Alternatives

Carpenter, P. A., and Eisenberg, P. Mental rotation and the frame of reference in blind and sighted individuals. *Perception & Psychophysics*, 1978, **23**, 117–24.

Pinker, S., and Finke, R. A. Emergent two-dimensional patterns in images rotated in depth. *Journal of Experimental Psychology: Human Perception and Performance*, 1980, **6**, 244–64.

Pylyshyn, Z. W. The rate of 'mental rotation' of images: A test of a holistic analogue hypothesis. *Memory & Cognition*, 1979, 7, 19–28.

17 Cognitive maps
Why do we get lost in space?

If you are asked to point in the direction of a distant city or suburb you will probably not regard the request as strange. Irrespective of the accuracy of your pointing, what is the nature of the knowledge that underlies this act? We can give directions to others on how to get to an unfamiliar location. How do they use this information to arrive there? When travelling in or to an unfamiliar city we frequently use maps to help us find our way. How do maps help us?

These are all questions about the nature of cognitive processes involved in geographical knowledge, that is, about 'cognitive maps'. Evans (1980), described the term 'cognitive map' as 'a general descriptor of the cognitive processes involved in the acquisiton, representation, and processing of information about actual physical settings' (p. 259).

Despite the practical importance of this topic, there is only limited research on the nature and function of cognitive maps. Probably the major difficulty hampering research lies in finding a technique that will reveal information about our cognitive maps uncontaminated by other factors. For example, the frequently used technique of map drawing suffers from a number of interpretive difficulties. Byrne (1979) and Evans (pp. 259–66) pointed out that individual differences in drawing ability may be spuriously interpreted as differences in cognitive maps. Evans pointed out that as well as being difficult to analyse, sketch map data are also difficult to interpret from a theoretical viewpoint. For example, if a person draws one set of points on a map 20 mm apart and another 40 mm apart, are we justified in assuming that the person means that the first set has half the separation of the second, or would it be more accurate to say that the first two points are simply judged as relatively closer, leaving precise ratios unspecified? Further, Byrne pointed out that drawing need not rely solely on exact geographical information represented in memory but can be inferred from known facts. These difficulties make it an unsatisfactory technique for understanding spatial cognition.

Byrne devised two methods for studying the mental representation of geographical knowledge which he implied did not rely on drawing skill. The first involved asking people the lengths of routes between two locations in a familiar area. These routes differed in terms of whether they were (a) in the centre of town or in the suburbs, (b) straight or involved changes in direction, and (c) of different lengths. Among other things, he found that estimates of length were increased for routes in the town centre and involving several changes in direction. In his second study subjects were asked to draw angles at which pairs of roads intersected. He found that the angles in subjects' drawings tended to deviate from the true angle and toward 90°.

Byrne argued that judgments of route length are probably influenced by the number of locations remembered on a route: the more locations, the longer the estimated length. He further argued that we use 90° for the angles of road intersections in our mental representations. He pointed out that both these results are consistent with the view that geographical knowledge is represented mentally as a 'network-map' rather than as a 'vector-map'. That is, our cognitive maps preserve the relative order of locations and turns but not absolute distance or angle information.

This workshop will replicate and extend Byrne's two experiments to determine how route length and road intersection information is represented in our cognitive maps.

General procedure

Data associated with both of Byrne's experiments can be collected in one session. You will need to obtain an accurate large-scale map of your local area which could be a city, a suburb, or even your campus.

For the first experiment you will need to choose a number of pairs of familiar locations from the map. Following Byrne, you could choose half of the routes in the business district and half in the residential part of town; half of the routes straight and half with changes in direction; and finally, routes of two different lengths. Your subject pool will probably be smaller than his so it would be advisable to have at least three comparison measures on each variable of interest. This would mean you will need to generate at least twenty-four comparisons: 2 (town centre v. periphery) × 2 (changed v. straight routes) × 2 (route lengths) × 3 (different comparisons for each combination of these variables).

Byrne used ratio scaling to obtain estimates of route lengths. This method requires subjects to make distance judgments in terms of a standard line representing a given distance. Subjects are asked to keep this distance in mind when making their estimates between locations (see Byrne, p. 149). Once you have familiarised subjects with the ratio scaling technique, they can proceed to make the distance estimates. Different subjects could have different random orders of the distance judgments.

In Byrne's second experiment subjects were asked to draw ten pairs of road junctions from memory 'paying particular attention to angles at which roads met' (p. 151), and omitting judgments on road intersections with which they were unfamiliar. You could follow Byrne and choose pairs of roads such that half of them meet at $60°-70°$ and half at $110°-120°$. Because the results of this experiment are important in understanding how environmental information is represented, and because of the difficulties arising from using a drawing technique in evaluating representation, it is suggested that you extend Byrne's procedure and add a different memory measure (e.g., a multiple-choice recognition test of road intersection angles). The network-map representation hypothesis would receive strong support if it could be shown that judgment errors with this measure approximate errors in Byrne's drawing procedure.

If you decide to include the recognition procedure, you could give half your subjects Byrne's drawing procedure, and the other half the recognition procedure. You will have to decide how to present the recognition material, how many alternatives should be presented, and how similar the angles in the alternatives should be.

It might also be interesting to extend the biographical data that Byrne collected from his subjects, by asking them how often and why they used the tested routes, and what mode of travel they normally used. You could either ask some general questions about subjects' use of cognitive maps, or ask them more specifically, how they made their judgments in your experiment.

In analysing the results of the first experiment you will need to work out the percentage distance error for each distance estimate, for each subject. A full analysis of the data would involve a three-way analysis of variance with repeated measures on each factor. However, if you lack the statistical expertise, it is sufficient to graph your data following Byrne (p. 149). This would give you some indication of the possible main effects and interactions.

You could examine your data from the second study in a similar way to Byrne by seeing whether the judged intersection angle deviates from the real angle and toward $90°$. Again, you could graph your results following Byrne (Fig. 2, p. 152). If you used a recognition test you would have to look not only at the number correct but also at the types of errors subjects made.

Do your results support Byrne's findings? Are there similar results from the two methods used to assess road angle intersection? If they are different, you should consider what implication this would have for Byrne's analysis of mental representation in cognitive maps. Do you think the ratio scaling method of assessing perceived distance is reasonable? Byrne did not specify the exact instructions to his subjects in the first experiment. Do you think subjects' performance could be affected by instructions? You could also discuss Byrne's suggestion that we acquire network-maps because of their functional value in helping us to find our way. It would be interesting to have your subjects introspect on what happens to their cognitive maps (network-maps?) when things on a familiar route change (e.g. a building is pulled down, traffic lights are erected, or a street becomes one-way). You could also consider under what circumstances we would acquire a vector-type cognitive map. What other kinds of information do we have represented in our cognitive maps?

Alternatives

From Byrne's first experiment it would seem that building density level has an effect on our judgment of distance: inner city routes with more buildings or locations on them were judged as longer. In an alternative experiment you could explore what other factors affect perceived distance. For example, does crossing a geographical boundary, such as a river, or crossing an emotional boundary, such as a sleazy part of town, affect perceived route length? You could also examine whether perceived route length correlates with the duration of the trip and the time of day travel takes place (e.g. in or out of the rush hour).

In his review paper, Evans raised a number of issues about the nature of our cognitive maps which could be investigated empirically. One issue that could be explored is the effect of familiarity with an environment on our cognitive maps. Evans (p. 275) claimed that although some existing research had controlled familiarity by equating it with the length of time (months, years, etc.) that people had been visiting a place, most research had ignored the role of environmental use factors. A university campus would be an ideal place to investigate this problem because you have access to subjects who have varying degrees of familiarity with the campus (as measured by time), as well as access to subjects who are differentially familiar with different parts of the campus. Such a study would allow you orthogonally to vary the time and the use factor.

Evans also pointed out that most of the research on cognitive maps has ignored performance effects associated with individual differences. Two exceptions to this general trend can be found in the work of Kozlowski and Bryant (1977) and Thorndyke and Stasz (1980), both of which are presented here as possible alternative workshops.

Kozlowski and Bryant were interested in the relationship between self-assessed sense of direction, and several performance measures. In one study, subjects rated their sense of direction, then completed three tasks: (a) pointing to five unseen buildings, (b) map-drawing of the university campus, and (c) pointing to north and to distant cities. Kozlowski and Bryant found that self-assessed sense of direction was positively related to the ability to indicate nearby locations, but was not related to the ability to indicate compass directions. They suggested that differences between those people with a good and those with a poor sense of direction might have been greater had judgments been made about less-familiar locations. This claim could be investigated by repeating their procedures using locations in a nearby town or suburb as stimuli rather than locations around a university campus. Subjects could imagine themselves at a location, facing in a certain direction, prior to indicating the direction of specified buildings.

In a further experiment Kozlowski and Bryant examined the performance of subjects with good and poor senses of direction on learning a novel environment, namely, a maze. On the first trial, subjects with differing self-assessed senses of direction were similar in their ability to point to the maze starting point. However, on subsequent learning trials only those subjects with a good sense of direction improved in their pointing ability. It would not be difficult to replicate this aspect of Kozlowski and Bryant's study since most places of higher education come fully equipped with mazes of corridors, interlocking rooms, and laboratories.

Two-dimensional maps are an indispensable aid to living in an urban environment. The method by which we understand and use maps raises several important issues. For example, do experienced map users use different cognitive processes to inexperienced map users, and can poor learners of map information be taught effective procedures and strategies to help their map learning?

Thorndyke and Stasz have looked at issues and questions such as these. They found that good map learners were superior to poor map learners in their ability to encode spatial information and in their ability to monitor what they had learned. In addition, good map users tended to adopt more successful learning procedures, such as dividing the map into sections and systematically learning the elements in each section. However, good map learners were not necessarily the most experienced map users. Subjects in a subsequent experiment who were instructed to use the successful learning procedures were able to reproduce a map more accurately after five learning trials than subjects not given these hints. They also found that subjects with good visual memory ability benefited more from the effective map learning procedure than did subjects with poor visual memory ability.

If you decide to replicate Thorndyke and Stasz's study, you will need to make a number of decisions contingent upon the time and resources you have available. You could dispense with their first study and simply use their data as a guide for constructing your training procedures. However, you might find experienced map users among senior geography students if you wanted to re-examine their first experiment. Rather than using three groups, you could compare the results of the effective training group with only one control group. If your time is restricted you could also cut down on the number of learning trials subjects receive.

Their study could be extended by seeing whether different kinds of cognitive processes are involved in learning different kinds of maps. For example, it would be interesting to see if people with high visual memory ability are better able to learn maps which are more visual in nature (e.g. a relief map), than people with low visual memory ability. Alternatively, you could see whether Kozlowski and Bryant's self-assessed sense of direction measure correlates with Thorndyke and Stasz's map learning tasks.

References

Byrne, R. W. Memory for urban geography. *Quarterly Journal of Experimental Psychology*, 1979, **31**, 147–54.

Evans, G. W. Environmental cognition. *Psychological Bulletin*, 1980, **88**, 259–87.

References for Alternatives

Kozlowski, L. T., and Bryant, K. J. Sense of direction, spatial orientation, and cognitive maps. *Journal of Experimental Psychology: Human Perception and Performance*, 1977, **3**, 590–8.

Thorndyke, P. E., and Stasz, C. Individual differences in the procedures for knowledge acquisition from maps. *Cognitive Psychology*, 1980, **12**, 137–75.

IV

Attention and pattern recognition

Introduction

The processes of remembering and imaging discussed in the first two sections of this book involved, but did not focus on, two further important and basic cognitive processes. These are the selection and interpretation of information. In this section we will be looking at research specifically concerned with these two processes under the headings of *attention* and *pattern recognition*. The topics are often linked in research and theories about cognitive processes. The very act of focussing or attending involves questions about when and how something is identified as a meaningful pattern.

In the research on attention, two main problems have been isolated. Firstly, while we are attending to one source of information, how much, if anything, of all the non-attended information are we taking in at the same time? The second problem concerns our ability to divide our attention. Can we focus on two or more sources of information at a time and how can we assess the role of attention in this situation?

The first problem above refers to what has been called 'selective' or 'focussed' attention. When you are at a party, you can listen to one person and generally ignore the other conversations around you. This example of focussed attention has been simulated in the laboratory using the 'dichotic listening technique' which is used in Workshop A1. Research with this technique demonstrates the limits of auditory attention. It has been adapted to the visual mode in a 'selective reading' paradigm which is illustrated in Workshop A2.

The research on focussed attention promoted a series of suggestions about which stage in processing the selection occurs. Broadbent's first 'filter model' proposed that the limit occurs early and is determined by physical characteristics of messages. However, this model does not account for the finding that our attention can be shifted to a non-attended message if the message has a special meaning, for example, if it contains our own name.

To account for this sort of example, Treisman developed an 'attenuator' model of selective attention. According to this model, one primary channel is attended to and the semantic information from other sources is attenuated or reduced. When a word on a non-attended channel is important or relevant, it is processed further. Deutsch and Deutsch suggested a further step, namely, that we extract meaning from *all* the incoming information, and that selective attention occurs 'late' in the process, just before response selection. Reviews of these models and their problems can be found in a number of books, for example, Glass, Holyoak, and Santa (1979), Kahneman (1973), Moates and Schumacher (1980), Norman (1976).

Each of the models mentioned above is tied to a view of the system as having sequential stages of processing, with a limit on processing at one of these stages. Recent research in both the memory and attention areas shows that such a view does not do justice to the complexity of these processes. Instead of assuming some structural limitation within the system, research workers such as Kahneman (1973) have stressed the overall processing capacity which subjects have for the demands of the tasks they perform. The limits of attention can then be viewed as a product of the amount of processing capacity and the structures used by tasks. This approach proves to be very useful in accounting for performance when attention is divided between two tasks, as illustrated in Workshop A3. The understanding of divided attention, as well as other attentional phenomena, has also been considerably advanced by the theoretical papers by Schneider and Shiffrin (1977) and Shiffrin and Schneider (1977). Their analysis of 'automatic' and 'controlled' processing has been influential in later discussions of the role of attention in cognitive processing models.

The remaining four workshops in this section are concerned with the problem of pattern recognition, although, as mentioned earlier, they also necessarily involve the selection of information.

Recognising patterns in sensory input is not limited to the visual modality. We identify patterns when we listen to speech, when we can recognise a number of odours, when we can identify objects by touch, and so on. However, most of the research has concentrated on the visual modality, and the workshops in this section follow this trend.

Models of human pattern recognition have been based on computer studies, on neurophysiological research and on findings from psychological experiments. There are good discussions of these approaches and of the general background of pattern recognition research in the books by Lindsay and Norman (1972), Reed (1973) and Rumelhart (1977), and in the selection of readings provided by Carterette and Friedman (1978) which covers both attention and pattern recognition. Some of the models which have been proposed are limited to explaining how we recognise units in isolation, for example, the letter *A*. However, we rarely face this sort of task in daily life. More often we need to recognise objects in a context, e.g. an *A* in handwriting within a word or a sentence. Neisser (1967) illustrated this context effect by asking subjects to locate particular target letters or words in lists. The lists varied in their degree of visual or semantic similarity to the targets. Subjects were faster to locate a target when the surrounding items were dissimilar. This task, referred to as 'visual search', is the subject of Workshop A4. Visual search is involved in the everyday problem of searching, for example, for a number or a name in a telephone book or in an index, or searching for a face in a crowd.

One of the basic questions of pattern recognition research is how we identify visual patterns as objects, faces, alphabetical letters, etc., or sound patterns as speech, in spite of the enormous variation in the sensory input within any one of these categories. If you think of the variety of different visual forms which you can label 'animal', you can see the scope of the problem. It is the specification of the limits of a concept which poses such problems for programming computers to recognise patterns — and incidentally highlights what extremely efficient pattern recognisers human beings are! Classifying a pattern as one of a category, for example, as a letter, would usually be assumed to occur *after* an item was identified, for example as an *A*. Workshop A5 suggests that this is not necessarily so. When subjects inspect an array for a particular target, they can classify items as belonging to a category (e.g. digits) without identifying each item individually. This category effect in visual search is an intriguing aspect of pattern recognition, and, as our A5 Alternatives section shows, has been found for words and faces as well as for alphanumeric stimuli.

The problem of how people classify a stimulus as a member of a category is taken up in Workshop A7. Reed (1978) considered this question in an overview of psychological studies of pattern recognition. He discussed the research which uses 'artificial' categories (experimenter-designed, e.g. dot patterns), and 'natural' categories (from the real world, e.g. plants, colours). One approach to the problem of classifying exemplars of both these types of categories is to assume that there is a central tendency or 'prototype' against which exemplars can be matched. The main experiment in Workshop A7 explores a related question of whether the boundaries of natural categories are 'fuzzy', i.e. ill-defined.

Finally, a question of interest concerns the recognition of patterns by specialists in particular areas. For example, chess masters can reproduce the state of play in a chess game more accurately than novices. The experience of the chess masters leads to the superior encoding and retrieval of the pattern of chess pieces. Musicians are another specialist group, skilled in recognising particular patterns. Workshop A6 investigates why musicians are superior to non-musicians in the task of reading and remembering music.

Each of these workshops focusses on the processes involved in attending to and interpreting sensory input. Both attention and pattern recognition are involved in language and thinking — the subjects of the following sections. As we have stressed in other sections, the division of cognitive processes into sections, as in this book, is often arbitrary and determined more by the specific focus of an investigation than by any noticeable divisions between the processes themselves.

References

Carterette, E. C., and Friedman, M. P. (eds). *Handbook of Perception* (vol. 9): *Perceptual Processing*. New York, Academic Press, 1978.

Glass, A. L., Holyoak, K. J., and Santa, J. L. *Cognition*. Reading, Mass.: Addison-Wesley, 1979.

Kahneman, D. *Attention and Effort*. Englewood Cliffs, N. J.: Prentice-Hall, 1973.

Lindsay, P. H., and Norman, D. A. *Human Information Processing: An Introduction to Psychology*. New York: Academic Press, 1972.

Moates, D. R., and Schumacher, G. M. *An Introduction to Cognitive Psychology*. Belmont, Calif.: Wadsworth, 1980.

Neisser, U. *Cognitive Psychology*. New York: Appleton-Century-Crofts, 1967.

Norman, D. A. *Memory and Attention: An Introduction to Human Information Processing* (2nd edn). New York: Wiley, 1976.

Reed, S. K. *Psychological Processes in Pattern Recognition*. New York: Academic Press, 1973.

Reed, S. K. Schemes and theories of pattern recognition. In E. C. Carterette and M. P. Friedman (eds). *Handbook of Perception* (vol. 9): *Perceptual Processing*. New York: Academic Press, 1978.

Rumelhart, D. E. *Introduction to Human Information Processing*. New York: Wiley, 1977.

Schneider, W., and Shiffrin, R. M. Controlled and automatic human information processing: I. Detection, search, and attention. *Psychological Review*, 1977, **84**, 1-66.

Shiffrin, R. M., and Schneider, W. Controlled and automatic human information processing: II. Perceptual learning, automatic attending, and a general theory. *Psychological Review*, 1977, **84**, 127-90.

A1 Focussed attention in listening

What do we hear at a cocktail party?

Recall for a moment what it is like to be at a party. You can listen to one conversation at a time and generally ignore the others going on around you. Yet you are aware of the general noise: you certainly notice when a momentary silence falls. You are also very likely to hear your name in a nearby conversation. How do we selectively attend to one voice and how much do we take in of the other conversations? As Norman (1976) points out, Cherry was the first to refer to this as 'the cocktail party problem'.

To study the problem in a controlled laboratory setting, Cherry devised a technique called 'dichotic listening'. Subjects hear two messages at once, either one to each ear through headphones, or from spatially separated loudspeakers. They are asked to focus on one message only, and in order to ensure that they are attending, they are asked to 'shadow' that message, that is, to repeat each word or item aloud as they hear it. While they are focussing on one message, the other can be varied to see what characteristics of this unattended message are processed. For example, its physical characteristics can be varied by changing it from a man's to a woman's voice; its semantic characteristics can be changed by varying the language in which the message is spoken, e.g. from English to French. It has usually been found that subjects notice physical changes in the non-attended ear, but not semantic or meaning changes. However, subjects do notice familiar material, e.g. their own name.

Both Kahneman (1973) and Norman (1976) review the theories and experimental evidence about selective attention. Much of the research has revolved around three approaches. The first (and earliest historically) favours the view that the selection of incoming information occurs *early* in the stages of processing, that is, emphasising the physical differences between messages as a basis for selection. The second is a modified version of the first, suggesting that non-attended messages are not completely blocked but are attenuated so that some material, e.g. material that is familiar or relevant, may be processed. The third view favours *late* selection of incoming information, that is, on the basis of meaning, after all the information has been automatically processed.

The aim of this workshop is to investigate these approaches to selective attention by establishing what we process of non-attended messages in a dichotic listening task.

General procedure

You will need a stereo tape recorder with separate volume controls for each channel, and headphones (or two separate speakers if you are going to test in a group situation). Subjects will be asked to shadow a message they hear in one ear (e.g. the right). They are then asked questions about the message to the other non-attended ear to establish which characteristics or changes in it they noticed.

Your first task then is to record pairs of messages. The ones to be shadowed can be selected from a book, each taking about one minute to read out. Record these on one channel and pair each with a message on the other channel to go to the non-attended ear. Time this non-attended message to start about five seconds after the attended ear message and to finish about five seconds earlier.

Your background reading should provide many ideas on the sort of variables you might test on the non-attended ear. You could change the physical characteristics of the message, e.g changing the voice from a man's to a woman's in the middle of the message, or introducing a buzzer sound at random during the message. The semantic characteristics of the message could be changed by varying the language in which the message is being spoken, or by changing it from meaningful prose to a string of unrelated words read out as prose, etc.

If you have access to cubicles interconnected for sound, you can play the tape to subjects wearing headphones in the cubicles. They can shadow the attended ear by writing down the message as they hear it and then answering the questions on a response sheet after each one-minute trial. Written shadowing can also be used for group testing where messages come over two spatially separated speakers, placed each side at the front of the class. If you test subjects individually, using a tape recorder and headphones, they can shadow the message aloud.

Subjects would be instructed to attend in each trial to the message you indicate — e.g. in the left ear, ignoring the message in the other ear — and to repeat aloud (or write down) as accurately as they can, what they hear word by word. Subjects may find the task difficult at first so have a practice tape with a passage of three to four minutes to one ear only so that they can get used to shadowing. Tell them it is essential that they try and repeat every word they hear of the attended message, but not to worry if they do stumble — they should pick it up again as soon as they can. Accurate shadowing is essential to ensure that the subjects' attention was completely taken up by the attended passage (although this is an assumption which probably depends on the difficulty of shadowing and which you might discuss after your experiment).

After subjects have had practice at shadowing, you can give them a series of experimental trials, say six varying physical variables in the non-attended message and six varying semantic characteristics, presented in random order. To check on whether subjects remember the content or notice the changes in the non-attended message, you can ask them at the end of each trial some non-directive questions (set out on pre-prepared response sheets) such as 'What occurred in your right ear?' or 'Can you report anything about the content of either message?' You can also give the subjects a sheet with a list of words on it, half of which were in the unattended message and the other half as distractors. Ask subjects to circle the words which they thought came from the message in the ear they were not attending to, guessing if they are not sure.

To collate your results, select those trials on which subjects made few, if any, shadowing errors, and summarise for those trials how much they recalled and recognised of the non-attended message. Is there any evidence that they noticed physical but not semantic changes? Is there any change in their response patterns after the first trial, when they then knew what you would be asking them? What bearing do your findings have on early versus late selection? How reasonable is the assumption that subjects' attention was completely taken up by the attended message?

Alternatives

Moray (1969) suggested that emotional content may be more likely to be noticed than neutral content in the non-attended passage. You could test this by composing a passage, for example, about university students failing examinations, being unable to get jobs, foreseeing gloomy prospects for the future, etc. Compare subjects' recall or recognition of its content with that for a neutral non-attended passage.

Objections have been raised to the use of auditory shadowing in experiments which aim to assess the extent of the processing of non-attended material. Bookbinder and Osman (1979) suggest the alternative of button-pressing to target words and you could adapt their method, e.g. by using finger-tapping instead of button-pressing and having the experimenter simply note against the list of words when each tap occurs.

Combining this with Moray's suggestion, you could see whether emotional content is more likely to be noticed than neutral content in the non-attended material. Would the rate of detection for secondary targets using button-pressing (or finger-tapping) be increased for emotionally toned words (e.g. 'exam' or 'fail' for university students)? If this does happen, you would need to check whether it occurs at the expense of primary target detection. Would these findings be predicted from Bookbinder and Osman's theoretical conclusion?

80   *Attention and pattern recognition*

References

Kahneman, D. *Attention and Effort.* Englewood Cliffs, N. J.: Prentice-Hall, 1973, (Chs 1 and 7).

Norman, D. A. *Memory and Attention: An Introduction to Human Information Processing* (2nd edn). New York: Wiley, 1976, (Chs 2 and 4).

References for Alternatives

Bookbinder, J., and Osman, E. Attentional strategies in dichotic listening. *Memory & Cognition*, 1979, 7, 511–20.

Moray, N. *Listening and Attention*, Harmondsworth, Middlesex: Penguin, 1969.

A2 Focussed attention in reading

Do we read between the lines?

While we read, we make several visual fixations in each line of print and at each fixation we take in one or more words. But what about the words in our visual periphery that are not actually fixated? Are words on adjacent lines also processed, perhaps influencing our processing or memory of the fixated words?

This possibility has been explored using a technique called 'selective reading'. Subjects are asked to read a passage aloud. Between the lines of the passage is another story or string of words. Subjects commonly recall little of this unattended material except that most notice their own name if it occurs there.

This finding is analogous to that for the selective listening technique in which subjects can selectively attend to one of two spoken messages, presented simultaneously but on some occasions words from the unattended passage, e.g. their own name, are noticed. It has also been claimed in selective listening experiments that though subjects cannot recall the unattended material, it nevertheless influences their comprehension of the attended passage.

Willows and MacKinnon (1973) suggested that the same effect may be shown in selective reading. Their experiment, on which this workshop is based, examined the hypothesis that the content of the 'unattended' material printed between the lines of the relevant passage may influence subjects' understanding even though they may not be able to recall the irrelevant material.

Willows and MacKinnon tested subjects' comprehension of the attended material by asking them to answer multiple-choice questions after reading each passage aloud. The choices for each question included a correct answer based on the material in the attended lines and an incorrect answer based on the information in the irrelevant lines. Choosing the latter would indicate an influence of the unattended on the attended material.

General procedure

You will need several prose passages for subjects to read. Each can be typed with double spacing and would occur in two conditions: in the selective reading condition, words would be printed between the lines of passage; in the control condition, there are non-words between the lines, i.e. collections of random letters, grouped to look like words. (Willows and MacKinnon's control condition had empty spaces between the attended lines; this would not ensure that the only way the selective attention conditions differed from the control was the presence of meaningful but irrelevant material in the unattended lines.)

The relevant lines can be typed in black and the irrelevant in red, or vice versa, as in Experiment 1 of Willows and MacKinnon, or, following their Experiment 3, all the typing of both relevant and irrelevant lines can be in black (irrelevant could be in italic type), with five red X's marking the beginning of the irrelevant lines. You can decide whether to have repetitions of words in the unattended lines or another passage of similar content, e.g. the attended passage could be on flower arrangement and the unattended could be on indoor plants or any other related topic. A further suggestion is to examine the effect of significant versus non-significant words in the non-attended lines, e.g. for university students significant words could be 'exam', 'fail', 'study', etc., or simply their own or familiar names.

The passages for selective attention and control conditions would need to be of comparable difficulty if each subject is tested for both conditions. However, if you use an independent groups design, then the same passage can be used under both conditions. For each passage, you will need multiple-choice comprehension questions. Each question should have one correct answer from the attended passage, one wrong 'intrusion' answer from the irrelevant passage and two or more other wrong but plausible answers: see Willows and MacKinnon (p. 295) for an example set.

If time and facilities permit, individual testing could be carried out, with subjects reading the passages aloud. An alternative is to ask subjects to read in a whisper in a group situation. If you adopt this 'whisper reading' procedure, you should stress to subjects that they read the relevant stories and turn to their questions on the passage immediately they have finished reading it. Whichever testing method you use, subjects can be told that the experiment concerns reading comprehension and that they will be asked to read a passage and answer questions about its content. They should be warned that on alternate lines with red X's at the beginning, there are letters or words to distract them. You could emphasise that they should not pay any attention to these lines but read their passage at their most comfortable speed, remembering that they will be asked questions about it. You might begin with one or two practice passages and questions to ensure that subjects are familiar with the task.

When you correct subjects' responses to the comprehension questions, pay special attention to the number of intrusion errors and the number of other errors. You can work out, for each of these measures, averages for the control and selective attention passages. Although these comprehension errors seem the most useful response variables, you could check on any other response measures you consider important. Willows, for example, also records reading speed, reading errors, and time taken to answer the comprehension questions. You could see whether there was an overall decrement in performance on these measures for the selective attention condition due to general interference from the non-attended message.

In discussion you could consider how similar the selective reading and selective listening tasks really are. What factors affect performance in the two situations? Can you make any statement from your results or those of Willows and MacKinnon on the role of peripheral visual input in the reading process?

Alternatives

You could follow up a suggestion by Willows and MacKinnon that 'the effects of systematically varying the semantic similarity of the relevant and irrelevant "channels" should be assessed' (p. 303) by having them range from very close in meaning to barely related in meaning. If, as many argue, reading is a process of extracting meaning, then you might expect more intrusion errors from semantically similar than from phonologically similar non-attended material.

Perhaps you could check for the effects of location of the intrusion items. Consider, for example, Willows's passage (1974, p. 411). Will subjects only respond to Comprehension Question 1 with the intrusion 'transport drivers' if that intrusion phrase occurs in close proximity to the correct 'truck drivers', or is proximity unimportant? If proximity is important, you might also consider whether the intrusion item has more effect when it occurs in the non-attended line before or after the correct item in the attended line. You could also investigate how close the lines of print need to be. Clearly, experiments on these questions will be quite difficult to organise, so be sure you have sufficient resources before you attempt them.

You may prefer to find an answer to these questions by using single words rather than prose. Schaffer and LaBerge (1979) found increased latencies to categorising single words, when the word was flanked by semantically unrelated words to which the subjects were instructed not to attend. You could repeat their Experiment 1, perhaps using words from other categories than those used by Schaffer and LaBerge, to test the generality of their notion of automatic semantic processing of unattended 'flanking' words. It might be interesting to use different words for 'flankers' than for targets (cf. Schaffer and LaBerge's word lists, p. 425), and then include a recognition test of the unattended words to see whether automatic processing implies that material will not be remembered. You could also consider varying either the position or the number of flankers.

Another interesting alternative experiment, if you have access to readers whose ability can be or has been graded, would be to investigate differences between good and poor readers in their susceptibility to influence from irrelevant lines in the selective reading task, as Willows (1974) did. You could see if differences also occurred in the word-categorisation task. You might further consider giving these subjects pictures rather than words for the non-attended material, following Willows (1978). You could use passages rather than lists of words to increase the similarity to normal reading.

Reference

Willows, D. M., and MacKinnon, G. E. Selective reading: Attention to the "unattended" lines. *Canadian Journal of Psychology*, 1973, **27**, 292-304.

References for Alternatives

Schaffer, W. O., and LaBerge, D. Automatic semantic processing of unattended words. *Journal of Verbal Learning and Verbal Behavior*, 1979, **18**, 413-26.

Willows, D. M. Reading between the lines: Selective attention in good and poor readers. *Child Development*, 1974, **45**, 408-15.

Willows, D. M. Individual differences in distraction by pictures in a reading situation. *Journal of Educational Psychology*, 1978, **70**, 837-47.

A3 Divided attention

How many things can we attend to at once?

Are you one of those people who claim to be able to study while listening to the radio? Have you ever pondered whether you are attending to both stimuli or perhaps concentrating on one and monitoring the other? You may have noticed it was easier to study with music rather than with talking as the background accompaniment. This workshop is concerned with phenomena of this sort in the area called 'divided attention'.

This term has been applied in a general way to the processes involved when any two or more tasks are carried out at the same time, whether or not the tasks require concurrent responses or later memory. Compare the following three examples of subjects' behaviour: listening to a voice and watching slides (no concurrent overt response), shadowing a voice and watching slides (one concurrent response), or shadowing a voice and searching for a target word in a list (two concurrent responses). Memory for each of the components of these examples could be tested later. All three examples have been referred to as situations involving divided attention.

Two variables which may affect the success of attending to two tasks at once are the similarity and relative difficulty of the tasks. Kahneman (1973) has distinguished between these two sources of interference in divided attention. He suggests the term 'structural interference', to apply when the two tasks are similar (the example above of trying to read and listen to a talk on the radio) because 'the activities occupy the same mechanisms of perception or response' (p. 196). 'Capacity interference', on the other hand, can occur when either or both tasks are increased in difficulty (for example, compare a novice with a skilled car driver in their ability to converse while driving). Kahneman suggests that this sort of interference occurs 'as a function of the attentional demands of competing activities' (p. 196).

These two views can most usefully be regarded not as competing but as applying in different divided attention situations: the first where the similarity of the tasks is the main variable, and the second where the focus is on their relative difficulty.

This concept of two types of interference in attention tasks can help to elucidate some of the research findings in the area. For example, it has often been reported that when subjects shadow a message heard in one ear, they remember little or nothing of a concurrent message in the other ear. This finding has been interpreted as showing a limit to our capacity to process information from two sources at once. However, an alternative view is that because the two tasks are very similar, structural interference is occurring.

Allport, Antonis and Reynolds (1972) provide support for this reinterpretation. They investigated the conditions under which divided attention is possible by varying the degree of similarity of the concurrent tasks. Their subjects shadowed a message they heard in one ear (Task 1) while trying to memorise stimuli they were seeing or hearing at the same time (Task 2). The similarity of the two tasks was varied in three conditions by changing the verbal component of Task 2. When the Task 2 stimuli were words presented to the subject's other ear, the verbal component was high and the task was therefore very similar to shadowing. Intermediate similarity was achieved by presenting the words visually so that there was still a verbal component but the task used a different modality from shadowing. Low similarity between the tasks was achieved by presenting pictures to be memorised, i.e. non-verbal stimuli, again in a different modality. Allport *et al.* could thus examine divided attention for three conditions of task similarity.

This workshop is based on the procedure for Experiment 1 of Allport *et al.* We are investigating whether subjects can divide their attention more successfully between dissimilar tasks (e.g. shadowing and memorising pictures) than between very similar tasks (e.g. shadowing and memorising auditory words).

General procedure

This workshop involves three groups of subjects with individual testing, so it is probably advisable to have two or three experimenters working on it together.

Firstly, select three prose passages and record them on tape to be presented to a subject's right ear through headphones for shadowing. Each message should be about one minute long. Two will be practice passages and one an experimental passage.

Next you can prepare three kinds of competing memory stimuli: *words* (*auditory*) for which you need to record two sets of fifteen single words on tape, spoken at a rate of one every 3 seconds, to be presented to the subject's left ear; *words* (*visual*) which are two sets of fifteen words typed in upper case, each presented on a slide or card shown to the subject, again at the rate of one every 3 seconds; and *pictures* which are two sets of fifteen slides (holiday scenes would be satisfactory), presented to subjects at the same rate.

Divide your subjects into three groups, one for each type of memory stimulus. Two sets of each stimulus were mentioned above because for each group you need two measures of performance: one for divided attention when subjects memorise while shadowing, and a control with the memory task alone to give a base measure of performance on this task.

You will need a measure of how much subjects can remember in the divided and undivided attention conditions. So you will need two recognition sets per group, each with thirty items, i.e. the fifteen 'old' items already presented and fifteen 'new' or distractor items. They are presented to the subject straight after each trial in a random order and the subject circles 'Yes' (seen or heard before) or 'No' (not seen or heard before) for each item on a pre-prepared response sheet. The recognition test for each group is presented in the same way as for the experimental trial, i.e. by means of headphones for Group 1 and by means of card or slides for Groups 2 and 3.

The procedure, then, for subjects in Group 1 (words-auditory) is firstly two practice shadowing trials, then instructions that they are to listen to the words they will hear in their other ear and are to try and remember them for a later recognition test. Present the words and then the test. Then tell them they are to shadow a message in their right ear as accurately as they can while single words are again presented to their left ear. They will be tested for their memory of these words, but stress that they are to treat the shadowing task as the main one, that is, they are to keep shadowing correctly. The procedure for subjects in the other two groups can be based on this approach but substituting the relevant memeory stimuli.

One way of showing that we can divide attention successfully would be to show little or no difference in memory performance between the conditions with and without concurrent shadowing. You should compare memory for the words-auditory, the words-visual and the pictures. So for the subjects whose shadowing is fairly accurate, you can calculate mean errors in memory performance in divided and undivided attention conditions. You can then consider whether your results refute the idea that we cannot do two things at once as suggested by the 'single-channel hypothesis' (discussed by Allport *et al.*). How well are your results explained by their 'multi-channel hypothesis' (p. 233)? Does it make any difference to your conclusions if subjects do not remember the meaning of what they were shadowing?

Alternatives

If there are only two experimenters available for this workshop, you may prefer to test only two groups, e.g. the words–auditory and pictures groups. These would provide a good test of the hypothesis.

Referring back to the introductiory discussion of Kahneman's notions relating to the similarity and difficulty of two concurrent tasks, you could alter the emphasis of your experiment from examining structural interference to examining capacity interference by altering the difficulty of either task: e.g. compare performance on a concurrent task while shadowing familiar or difficult material, or increase the difficulty of the memory task (see Allport *et al.*, p. 228).

There is a good discussion by Norman (1976, p. 78) of an experiment investigating resource limits in this way. You could also consult Kahneman (Chap. 10) for further ideas.

The multi-channel hypothesis has been further refined by Rollins and Hendricks (1980). They showed that the extent of interference in the processing of two concurrent verbal messages depends on the similarity of the analyses required by the two tasks. For example, saying category names of words presented auditorily (Task 1, using acoustic and semantic processing) interferes more with detecting a visually presented word rhyming with a target word (Task 2a, also using acoustic processing), than with detecting a particular category word in a visual list (Task 2b, using visual and semantic processing). You could investigate this by following their Experiment 3.

In their discussion, Rollins and Hendricks (1980) suggest that the relatively small amount of interference between the semantic tasks (referred to above as Tasks 1 and 2b) may be because 'a single amodal semantic system can simultaneously handle two relatively simple semantic tasks as long as the total capacity of the semantic system is not exceeded' (p. 107). You could take up this point by pairing Task 2b with a more difficult version of Task 1 (e.g asking subjects to listen to a passage for a later test of its meaning). A demonstration of interference here would support the view that general capacity limitations as well as task-specific limitations are necessary to account for results in this area.

A further interesting aspect of divided attention referred to by Allport *et al.* (1972, p. 234), is the role played by skill in our ability to process two concurrent inputs. Hirst, Spelke, Reaves, Caharack, and Neisser (1980) maintain that divided attention is limited not by a fixed pool of capacity but by the individual's level of skill. You could investigate this either by providing subjects with some degree of practice at carrying out two concurrent tasks like reading and writing, or by comparing those already practised in some skill (e.g. typing), with those who are not. Your experiment will be limited only by the amount of time at your disposal or by the availability of skilled subjects.

References

Allport, D. A., Antonis, B., and Reynolds, P. On the division of attention: A disproof of the single channel hypothesis. *Quarterly Journal of Experimental Psychology*, 1972, **24**, 225–35.

Kahneman, D. *Attention and Effort*. Englewood Cliffs, N. J.: Prentice-Hall, 1973, Ch. 10.

References for Alternatives

Hirst, W., Spelke, E. S., Reaves, C. C., Caharack, G., and Neisser, U. Dividing attention without alternation or automaticity. *Journal of Experimental Psychology: General*, 1980, **109**, 98–117.

Norman, D. A. *Memory and Attention: An Introduction to Human Information Processing* (2nd edn). New York: Wiley, 1976.

Rollins, H. A., Jr., and Hendricks, R. Processing of words presented simultaneously to eye and ear. *Journal of Experimental Psychology: Human Perception and Performance*, 1980, **6**, 99–109.

A4 Visual search

How do we find what we are looking for?

A task familiar to everyone is searching through a page in the phone book for a particular number, e.g. having located the correct surname and not being sure of the initial, we search down the suburbs, keeping the relevant one in mind. We can sometimes search down the numbers themselves, knowing the target number begins, say, with 90. Another example of visual search would be scanning a list of index words looking for particular topics.

How do we perform such tasks? Do we just use visual information in these tasks, e.g. looking for visual features such as curved lines? How do we know when we have reached the item we want? Can we look for more than one target at a time just as easily as for one? The whole problem concerns the skill of visual search and pattern identification.

Neisser (1967), discussed some of the answers proposed to these questions. He referred to earlier experiments in which subjects scan down lists of letters for a target letter at an unpredictable position. The average time taken to find a letter varies as a function of the context: for example, it takes longer to find a 'K' among straight-line letters than among those with curved features like 'S' and 'C'. Neisser also found that after considerable practice at the task, subjects were just as fast locating any of ten target letters as they were locating only one.

Following these experiments with single-letter targets, Neisser and Beller (1965) reported two experiments in which the targets were words. They compared the search time required to locate three types of targets: firstly, a familiar word, e.g. 'Monday'; secondly, one of a familiar group of words, e.g. one of the American States; and thirdly, a target defined in terms of its meaning alone, e.g. 'an animal' or 'a person's first name'. Neisser and Beller suggested that the first two tasks involve 'stimulus examination' or processing of the physical properties of the stimuli, while the third also involves 'memory examination' or reference to stored semantic information.

This workshop is based on Experiment 1 of Neisser and Beller and examines the hypothesis that scanning will be faster when the target can be distinguished by stimulus examination alone than when its definition requires memory examination.

General procedure

You will need to decide first what sort of targets you will use to test the hypothesis – you can follow Neisser and Beller's experiment, or, better still, devise your own stimuli. Each target will be embedded in a list and there will have to be several lists for each target type. Neisser and Beller discuss how they compiled their lists using a computer, but several student experimenters can collaborate in preparing this workshop and share the task of devising the word lists so that they are drawn up reasonably quickly.

Lists of 50 words are a good length, i.e. 49 extra words plus the target word. Each list can be typed on a separate sheet, vertically down the page, with one word on each line. The pages can then be collated into booklet form. The target items are randomly positioned in each list.

Each subject is tested individually, so, depending on the time available in the laboratory session, you may need either to collect data beforehand and simply demonstrate the task in the session or have subjects working in pairs in class, taking turns to be experimenter and subject. (This would mean that you would need two sets of the lists: simply use the same 49 words of each list and slot in different targets.)

Chronoscopes or stopwatches are needed for timing the search of each list. On any trial, the experimenter tells the subject the target and then starts timing when the subject begins to search, stopping the timer when the target is located. You will need to prepare record sheets for experimenters to note down the time taken to search each list. It is suggested that you have 8 lists for each target type. Leave the first two trials as practice and score only trials 3 to 8 for each target type.

This might be an example of a record sheet:

Set 1 Target a.

List	Time	Position of target	Time Diff.	Position Diff.	Time per item
3	3 s	11	5 s	10	$\frac{5}{10} = 0.5$ s
4	8 s	21			

The procedure for calculating the average search time per item is as follows. For each target type, compare lists 3 and 4, 4 and 5, 5 and 6, 6 and 7, 7 and 8. Calculate the time difference between the two searches and the position difference, i.e. the number of lines separating the targets. To calculate the time per item, divide the time difference by the position difference. This may seem complicated but you will find it straightforward once you have your data. (Note that it is theoretically possible to get negative times per item: these can be ignored and omitted from final averages calculations.) For each subject, find the median search time per item for each target type. Then finally calculate the group average for each target type by finding the mean of these subject medians.

Is scanning time slower when memory examination is involved, as suggested by the hypothesis? When you look at Neisser and Beller's results, remember that they were examining the effect of practice on visual search performance over a six-week period. You can compare your data only with the initial trials of their study (p. 353).

Useful information could be gained by asking the subjects how they did the task. What role do sub-vocalisations play in their performance?

Alternatives

Although Neisser (1967) presented a model of visual search which emphasised the visual processes involved, subsequent research has shown that this is not always applicable: for example, acoustic factors can be involved, as demonstrated in the everyday example of repeating the target word to yourself as you search. Rabbitt (1978), in a thorough analysis of visual search, discussed studies which show this effect (pp. 107–9). For an alternative experiment, you could adopt the method of one of the studies he mentioned there, e.g. ask subjects to search through lists for targets varying in their acoustic similarity to the background stimuli. If you find an effect of acoustic factors on visual search, you could consider the implications for Neisser's theory, noting Rabbitt's point that practice in searching may remove the effect.

Other data inconsistent with Neisser's model were obtained by Brand (1971). She reported that for numeral targets, search through lists of other numerals was slower than search through letter lists. You could make up lists of letters and digits to test for this effect and refer again to Rabbitt (p. 100 ff.) for a discussion of this categorisation effect.

References

Neisser, U. *Cognitive Psychology*. New York: Appleton-Century-Crofts, 1967 (especially ch. 3).

Neisser, U., and Beller, H. K. Searching through word lists. *British Journal of Psychology*, 1965, **56**, 349–58.

References for Alternatives

Brand, J. Classification without identification in visual search. *Quarterly Journal of Experimental Psychology*, 1971, **23**, 178–86.

Rabbitt, P. Sorting, categorization, and visual search. In E. C. Carterette and M. P. Friedman (eds). *Handbook of Perception* (vol. 9): *Perceptual Processing*. New York: Academic Press, 1978, 85–134.

A5 Visual target classification

When is an O not an O?

When you look down an index in a book for a particular entry, you are engaging in visual search. If you start wondering what processes are involved in your searching, you might think that the visual features of the words you scan are important, that you are looking for a certain pattern of lines, and you recognise the entry you want on the basis of its physical features. This sort of model certainly fits a number of examples of visual search but it may not be the whole story. There are indications that in some visual search tasks, performance is based not only on characteristics of the stimulus but also on the category to which the searcher assigns the stimulus, e.g. letter versus digit. Several studies have found that subjects are generally faster scanning down an array of letters looking for a digit target than for a letter target. Subjects are also faster finding a letter than a digit target in an array of digits.

One way of describing this result is to say that in a visual search task, classifying items into categories is somehow easier than identifying what particular items they are. One possible explanation could still be in terms of physical features rather than symbolic categories, namely, that scanning results are due to differences in the physical features of the members of the categories, e.g. that letters have different distinctive features compared to digits. One way of testing this hypothesis is to equate the general physical features of each category closely. But this is difficult to do perfectly. So another test reported in an experiment by Jonides and Gleitman (1972) is particularly ingenious.

Jonides and Gleitman were interested in whether 'the category effect' is really based on conceptual differences or whether it is due to physical stimulus differences. They tested whether it still occurred when they controlled the physical characteristics of the target item. To do this, they used the very same physical target stimulus, the symbol 'O', in two different conceptual conditions. It was presented as a digit (called a 'zero') or as a letter (called O) in a field of either letters or digits. Instead of using visual search through long lists, displays of 2, 4 or 6 items were briefly presented to subjects and the dependent variable was the time they took to indicate whether a target was present or absent.

This workshop is based on the Jonides and Gleitman experiment and tests the hypothesis that subjects will be faster locating the symbol 'O' among letters when it is called 'zero' (i.e. a category difference) than when it is called O (a name difference) and faster locating it among digits when it is called O (category difference) rather than 'zero' (name difference).

General procedure

You will need a chronoscope and a tachistoscope or a projector with a fast time-shutter (for exposure times of 150 msec.) or, of course, a computer display screen if you have access to one. This workshop is best done with two experimenters for ease of running the experiment, especially if you are using a tachistoscope.

Subjects are divided into two groups. For Group 1, the search targets are the uppercase letters A, Z, and O (specified as the vowel O); for Group 2, the search targets are the digits 2, 4 and O (specified as zero). These targets (letters and digits) are presented in either an array of uppercase letters randomly chosen from the set (CEFHIJKLNPRSTUVXY), or an array of digits from the set (135689). Depending on the time available you can decide what array size you will use, or whether you will vary its size.

Each subject is given some practice trials (say 4) followed by test trials — 36 should be sufficient. Subjects in each group have half the trials with the target in a field of letters, and half when it is to be located in a field of digits. On half of all trials the target is present; on the other half it is absent. Subjects are asked on any trial to signal in one way (e.g. to press a switch to the right) as soon as they see the target and to signal in another way (e.g. to press the switch to the left) if it is not there. (You will probably not have enough subjects to have two groups, one responding to the presence of target, and the other to absence, as Jonides and Gleitman did).

All 36 trials should be presented in a random order. The design of the experiment then looks like this:

		Group 1 Letter target		Group 2 Digit target	
		No. of trials		No. of trials	
		A	6	2	6
	LETTERS	Z	6	4	6
		O	6	O	6
FIELD					
		A	6	2	6
	DIGITS	Z	6	4	6
		O	6	O	6

Record sheets prepared beforehand will make scoring easier. Tell the subject the target name and give a signal before each trial (e.g. 'Two, ready!'

or 'Z, ready!'). The timer is started by the onset of the stimulus field and the subject's decision reaction time is recorded.

The average time taken to respond correctly for the presence of each target type in both fields can be calculated. Compare the reaction times for targets A and Z, and for 2 and 4 for same and different category fields with the reaction times for the targets O as a vowel or O as a digit in these two types of field.

Do your results show a category effect, supporting Jonides and Gleitman's findings? In discussion, you could consider their two suggested hypotheses for explaining the effect. Can you think of ways to test between them experimentally? You might speculate on what the features might be which Jonides and Gleitman mentioned as defining category membership and identity (p. 459).

Alternatives

In a between-category search (e.g. for a digit among letters), subjects may process each item less fully than in a within-category search (e.g. for a digit among other digits). This is the 'partial processing hypothesis' suggested by Gleitman and Jonides (1976). They found evidence that 'categorization has a cost' (p. 283), in that less information is registered and/or retained in between- than in within-category search. You could explore this cost, either for the field items, using a recognition test of stimulus cards after completing visual search trials, or for the target items, using catch trials of items which are incorrect but of similar category to targets.

You could use more complex stimuli, such as words or faces, to investigate category effects. For example, are subjects quicker at finding a target word such as 'corgi' in a list of words from a different category, e.g. colours, than in a list of same category words, in this case, types of dogs? One of the controls necessary in such an experiment is to ensure that any result is not accounted for by physical rather than semantic differences between target and background. Henderson and Chard (1978) took this into account by controlling word length and graphemic similarity of target and background. You could repeat their Experiment 1, with subjects searching for a target through lists of words with varying category resemblance to the target words.

The problem of recognising a familiar face, e.g. when you are waiting at a station barrier to meet a friend coming off a train, has been modelled by Bruce (1979) in a series of interesting visual search experiments. Her stimuli were photographs of faces, and she included a slightly different response measure from the above studies, namely rejection latencies for different types of distractor items. She found distinct category effects, similar to those for words. For example, when the target was a photograph of a well-known politician, subjects were slower to reject faces of other politicans than those of actors, when all the distractors were visually similar to the target.

You could collect photographs from newspapers and magazines of local well-known faces, e.g. in politics or television, and test the generality of Bruce's impressive category effect. Incidentally, you might note that she used only female subjects. Remember to control factors such as visual similarity and familiarity, or manipulate them as Bruce did.

For an alternative set of experiments, you could explore the characteristics and relationships of the two categories used as targets and distractors. For example, instead of using politicians and actors, you could use politicians from two political parties or from two countries, provided they are likely to be sufficiently well known to your subjects. Would you still expect to obtain a category effect? As the degree of between- and/or within-category relationships increases, you could investigate whether there is an increase in overall rejection times. Such a result might be predicted from a possible increase in the time taken for semantic analysis steps in the model suggested by Bruce (Figure 4, p. 387). On the other hand, perhaps the category effect remains constant as long as subjects can provide a distinctive label for each category.

You might also consider the general theoretical implications of all this research for models of visual search, particularly for the distinction between identification and categorisation. Bruce is a good source here in her analysis of possible models (pp. 385–8) and in the general discussion at the end of her paper.

Reference

Jonides, J., and Gleitman, H. A conceptual category effect in visual search: O as letter or as digit. *Perception & Psychophysics*, 1972, **12**, 457–60.

References for Alternatives

Bruce, V. Searching for politicians: An information-processing approach to face recognition. *Quarterly Journal of Experimental Psychology*, 1979, **31**, 373–95.

Gleitman, H., and Jonides, J. The cost of categorization in visual search: Incomplete processing of targets and field items. *Perception & Psychophysics*, 1976, **20**, 281–8.

Henderson, L., and Chard, J. Semantic effects in visual word detection with visual similarity controlled. *Perception & Psychophysics*, 1978, **23**, 290–8.

A6 Recognising musical patterns

When musicians read musical notes, do they always hear the sound of music?

One of the interesting aspects of memory lies in studying the differences between specialists and novices in areas of skilled performance. It has been shown, for example, that chess masters' memory for positions in a chess game is superior to that of inexperienced chess players, but that the two groups do not differ in their memory for randomly placed chess pieces.

Another area of skilled performance involving memory concerns the sight-reading ability of musicians. Sight-reading involves three aspects: rapid recognition, memory of musical notation and the ability to translate this information into motor behaviour. Sloboda (1976) investigated the second of these by comparing the ability of musicians and non-musicians to recall musical notation. He presented notes on a stave and after an interval asked subjects to reproduce (i.e. draw) the notes they had seen. Sloboda found there was no difference in the recall of musicians and non-musicians when the stimuli had been shown for a very short time (e.g. 20 msec.). However, musicians recalled significantly more notes than non-musicians when the exposure time was 150 msec. or more.

Sloboda concluded that both musicians and non-musicians encode the notes visually at brief stimulus durations but that a second non-visual code comes into operation for musicians when the exposure time is increased beyond 150 msec. This second code used by musicians could be a 'naming' code since all musical notes have alphabetical names, or it could be a 'pitch' or acoustic code: the sounds of the notes could be registered by musicians.

In two further experiments, Sloboda investigated the sort of code used by musicians by attempting to show an effect of various 'interference' stimuli on their memory for notes. Usually these stimuli are given to subjects while the test stimulus is being presented and/or in the interval between presenting a stimulus and asking for its recall. However, Sloboda (Experiment 3) played tapes of either music or someone speaking as continuous background interference during both presentation and recall of the musical notation, to test whether subjects were encoding and storing the notation as sounds (i.e. musical tones or letter names). If the notation was being acoustically encoded, recall should be poorer in these conditions than in a no-interference condition.

Although musicians were better able to remember the musical notation, his results showed no effect of any of the interference conditions on either musicians' or non-musicians' performance. He concluded that either musicians do not encode visually presented notes by their names or pitches, or that they can carry on concurrent activities with the same code simultaneously.

However a further possibility is that his experiments were not optimally designed to investigate the question. It may improve the interfering effect on musicians' coding processes to use single notes or letters rather than continuous music or speech and to present them in the interval between stimulus presentation and recall rather than having continuous background interference.

This workshop incorporates these ideas in a modified version of Sloboda's Experiment 3 to test whether musicians encode musical notation using naming or pitch codes.

General procedure

The selection of subjects is important for this workshop. You will need a group of musicians who are experienced sight-readers and another group of people of roughly the same age who are not musicians and do not sight-read. A difference in musical experience and knowledge between the two groups ensures a difference in memory for musical notation. (This requirement of some specialist subjects may mean you need to obtain them from outside your laboratory group but you could still use your class as the non-expert group.)

Your stimulus presentations need to show a stave with six notes. The positions of the notes are randomly determined. If you have a tachistoscope, you could use one field to present a stave and another field for the cards with six notes so that on each trial the subject sees the notes superimposed on the stave. The stimulus should be presented for two seconds. If you do not have access to a tachistoscope, you could draw stave and notes on cards and show them one at a time in front of the subject. Alternatively, you could use an overhead projector to present the stimuli for group testing and time each presentation for 2 seconds with a stopwatch. (Whichever method you choose, it is recommended that for ease of running the experiments, two experimenters collaborate on this workshop.)

You could draw up a series of response sheets, each with a musical stave drawn on it, for subjects to draw in the notes they recall after each trial. Make sure in practice trials that the non-musicians understand that notes either cover only one stave line or fill the space between two lines.

The sequence of events on any trial would then be: presentation of stimulus card followed by an interference condition, and, finally, reproduction by the subject on a response sheet of as many of the stimulus notes as he or she can recall.

There are three sorts of interference you could use: auditory tones (to test for a possible pitch code), spoken letters (for a naming code) and visual pattern (for a visual code). For the auditory tones interference, instead of using a recording of a violin concerto or other music as Sloboda did, you could consider recording sets of six notes randomly selected played on a piano or other instrument and presented to subjects through headphones or over speakers. For the interference to a naming code, you will need a second set of recordings, this time of someone speaking letters (A to G only), again, say, six per trial. For the visual pattern interference, cards similar to the stimulus set could be used, i.e. with stave and a different set of six notes. You need to ensure that the three interference conditions are of equal duration. Pilot work will help you decide the appropriate retention interval. Longer retention intervals may increase any differences between musicians and non-musicians.

Ten trials for each interference condition and an extra 10 trials with no interference (simply an interval of equivalent length between stimulus and memory test) should be sufficient. This gives 40 experimental trials in all, ideally with trials blocked by condition but with blocks randomly ordered. Of course, with group testing it will not be possible to randomise completely, in which case care should be taken to treat the musicians and non-musicians similarly. After collecting your data it might be informative to ask subjects about any strategies they were using.

With two groups, musicians and non-musicians, and with each subject tested in all conditions the design would be as follows:

	NO INTERFERENCE	NOTES	INTERFERENCE CONDITIONS LETTERS	PATTERN
MUSICIANS				
NON-MUSICIANS				

You can calculate the mean number of notes correctly recalled for each condition and compare your pattern of results with Sloboda's. You might also like to take a more detailed look at your data, to determine the types of errors that subjects make. For example, do subjects recall the correct pattern of the notes on the stave but misplace that pattern (e.g. move all six notes up two steps)? Is there any difference in the types of errors made by musicians and non-musicians, and is there any relationship between the type of error and interference condition?

Discussion of the experiment could include considering whether the selective interference method is a good way of answering the question how musicians code musical notes. Did their reports to you after the experiment reveal the strategies they used? Do your results support Sloboda's idea that 'particularly well-learned kinds of material may reside in special memory areas' (p. 14)? Is this an appropriate method for testing this idea anyway? Would it make a difference if the notes made up a proper musical phrase?

Alternatives

There are quite a few variations to the basic procedure outlined above which would provide a test of Sloboda's idea that musicians use special coding strategies. For example, you could vary the exposure time, the retention interval between presentation and test, the number and configuration or contour of the notes and the extent to which the visual stimulus resembled normal music (i.e. with clef signs, key signatures, accidentals and normal rhythmic notation present). In a subsequent experiment Sloboda (1978) systematically varied the configuration of the notes on the stave. He found that the recall differences between musicians and non-musicians increased for patterns with straight-line contours or few direction changes (familiar patterns in normal music), indicating that musicians were making use of different memory and/or pattern recognition strategies. These strategies might not be appropriate with random note sequences.

It may be that musicians can use any or all of pitch, naming or visual codes, depending on the situation at any one time: so that when one code is not going to be effective, another process is switched in. For example, naming would not be useful if the subject expected a letter interference task, so he or she might switch to a pitch code. Think of ways of testing this possibility, taking into account the way expectations can be produced about any trial in an experiment by the sort of trials the subject has immediately before that trial.

Sight-reading single notes on one stave is a relatively easy task compared to that faced by a pianist who must monitor two staves at a time, scanning vertically as well as horizontally. Wolf's (1976) analysis of sight-reading suggests that one difference between good and bad sight-readers amongst musicians could lie in their ability to recognise patterns rapidly and to combine vertical and horizontal information. If you can find some musicians who will acknowledge that they are poor sight-readers, you could test this proposal using Sloboda's basic procedure. Wolf makes some other interesting suggestions that could be explored as well.

Another way to investigate the codes used by musicians and non-musicians is to present melodies auditorally rather than visually. For example, Dowling (1978) found that 'contour' was also an important feature in aural recognition of melodies by both musicians and non-musicians. Musicians, however, seem able to code more detailed information about melodic patterns since, unlike non-musicians, they are able to differentiate melodies with the same contour but different relative interval sizes between notes. Some knowledge of music is probably an essential prerequisite for work in this area, but it would certainly be interesting to explore Dowling's ideas. Here again you could systematically vary the configuration of the notes in the melody and compare the effects of these variations on the performance of musicians and non-musicians. If you are unfamiliar with the signal detection methodology used by Dowling, you could simply use a same/different recognition task and score the number of correct judgments.

Reference

Sloboda, J. A. Visual perception of musical notation: Registering pitch symbols in memory. *Quarterly Journal of Experimental Psychology*, 1976, **28**, 1-16.

References for Alternatives

Dowling, W. J. Scale and contour: Two components of a theory of memory for melodies. *Psychological Review*, 1978, **85**, 341-54.

Sloboda, J. A. Perception of contour in music reading. *Perception*, 1978, **7**, 323-31.

Wolf, T. A cognitive model of musical sight-reading. *Journal of Psycholinguistic Research*, 1976, **5**, 143-71.

A7 Concepts and categorisation
Is baldness a fuzzy category?

Think for a moment about the two statements 'a robin is a typical bird' and 'a penguin is a typical bird'. The first statement seems somehow more true than the second. It suggests that a robin is a bird par excellence, that it possesses attributes which make it a good representative of those given the label 'bird'. A penguin, on the other hand, is far from a central member of that class. It does not fly, it swims rather like a fish, and looks like a man in a dinner suit. In fact, it is only with some difficulty that we think of a penguin as a bird at all.

When we assign things to a class (i.e. give them a general label like 'bird'), we are classifying or categorising, or using a concept. This is an important and pervasive aspect of thought in that it serves to reduce the diversity of input we need to deal with, and thereby enables us more readily to relate new instances to our existing knowledge structure. An analysis of the use and structure of categories addresses the whole question of how we acquire and store knowledge.

How are categories formed and how do they operate? Answers to these questions have traditionally been sought by studying artificial, experimenter-defined categories, for example, geometrical figures varying in colour, size, shape, etc. Using this type of category means that those factors which might affect the development and use of a category (e.g. the frequency with which instances are encountered), can be controlled or manipulated and the structure and features of a category can be precisely specified.

However, such control is not possible with 'natural' categories. These are collections of objects in our environment which we treat as equivalent at some level and to which we can give a single name, e.g. cat, furniture. Rosch (1978) has carried out a considerable amount of theoretical analysis and empirical research on the question of categorisation, particularly with regard to natural categories. She has considered several aspects of the internal structure of natural categories. For example, she suggested that some members of a category are more typical or representative of the category than others. In other words, there are varying degrees of category membership, with 'prototypes', according to Rosch, being the best representatives of categories. For some artificial categories it is possible actually to specify one exemplar as the prototype, but for natural categories the prototype is a more abstract notion, with exemplars of the category being conceptualised at different distances from this central measure.

A further important hypothesis about natural categories made by Rosch is that their boundaries are usually ill-defined, so there is no clear definition of category membership and non-membership. For example, how would you decide if a pogo-stick is a vehicle? Other models of natural as well as artificial categories have assumed that category boundaries are clear and unequivocal.

McCloskey and Glucksberg (1978) carried out an experiment to test directly whether natural categories are well-defined or 'fuzzy'. Subjects were asked to decide whether or not an instance was a member of a category. McCloskey and Glucksberg took the degree of between-subject disagreement and within-subject inconsistency to indicate the fuzziness of categories. They found that subjects disagreed with each other and were inconsistent in their decisions about exemplars which were of intermediate typicality for a category (e.g. *pogo-stick–vehicle*). On the other hand, items which were either highly typical (e.g. *car–vehicle*) or highly atypical of a category (e.g. *table–vehicle*) led to reliable decisions between and within subjects. McCloskey and Glucksberg concluded that the inconsistency and disagreement shown by their subjects for items on the border of category membership (i.e. those neither clearly members or non-members) indicated that natural categories are fuzzy rather than well-defined. This workshop is based on their experiment.

General procedure

Your first choice might be whether you replicate McCloskey and Glucksberg's experiment in full, or look at just one of their between- or within-subject consistency measures. To investigate between-subject variation in decisions, you will need only one testing session, but for the within-subject consistency measure, you will need to arrange two testing sessions separated by at least a week. McCloskey and Glucksberg included the within-subjects analysis to check that between-subjects disagreement did not simply reflect differences between subjects in their boundaries for well-defined categories. A decision to omit the within-subjects test would, on their reasoning, limit your conclusions about category boundaries. You could, however, examine the pattern of between-subject responses and you may even consider that fuzziness of categories is sufficiently indicated by variability in category boundary placements between the members of a group.

To reduce testing time and data analysis, select some of the 18 categories used by McCloskey and Glucksberg (pp. 467–71), or some new categories. You will also need to decide how many exemplars to use for each category. The number of categories and exemplars you choose depends, in part, on the time you have available. Note that some 'exemplars' of a category should clearly not be members of the category at all (e.g. *salmon–insect*) and that for each category, you need equal numbers of exemplars covering the same range of typicality.

You will need two groups of subjects. For Group 1 (category membership decisions) you could follow McCloskey and Glucksberg's procedure for setting up booklets containing lists of exemplar-category name pairs, for example, *apple–fruit*, with the response letters 'Y' (yes), 'N' (no), and 'U' (unfamiliar) beside each pair. Subjects are asked to circle one of these to indicate their decision on whether the first word of the pair is a member of the category specified by the second word. 'Unfamiliar' is used for words they cannot understand or which they consider to be ambiguous (see McCloskey and Glucksberg's instructions, p. 463). If you decide to look at within–subjects inconsistencies, the subjects in Group 1 would be tested twice, with at least one week between testing occasions.

Subjects in Group 2 (typicality ratings) are given lists of the same categories and exemplars as Group 1, but with the category name at the top, and possible exemplars listed below. They are asked to rate each exemplar for its degree of typicality of the category. You might decide to dispense with Group 2 and just use the typicality ratings given by McCloskey and Glucksberg.

The first step in analysing your data is to remove from all analyses those pairs for which any subject in Group 1 circled 'U'. Then for all remaining exemplar-category pairs, you can calculate the mean percentage of 'yes' responses. Using either the typicality ratings provided by Group 2, or those reported by McCloskey and Glucksberg, you could then calculate the mean percentage 'yes' responses for each of several levels of typicality, perhaps grouping the levels in the way McCloskey and Glucksberg did in Table 1 (p. 464). You could follow their Figure 1 and plot mean percentage 'yes' against typicality level. To show the extent of between-subject agreement, you could adopt their method of determining the proportion of nonmodal responses and graph these against typicality level. Analysis of variance on the decisions at different typicality levels would show the statistical significance of any differences you find.

Do your data show the same pattern as McCloskey and Glucksberg's? What evidence do you have that the categories you used have fuzzy rather than well-defined boundaries? Were both common and rare items at intermediate typicality levels just as likely to be classified inconsistently, as McCloskey and Glucksberg found? In discussion, you could also consider which of the alternative models of category representation in semantic memory, discussed by McCloskey and Glucksberg, seems to be the most appropriate. Rosch and her co-workers frequently stated that their concern is with the *structure* of categories, rather than with the *processes* involved in their use. Do you agree with Rosch 'that the facts about prototypes can only constrain, but do not determine, models of representation' (p. 40)?

Alternatives

Instead of using concrete objects, you could use other types of categories, e.g. abstract categories such as beauty, goodness, faith, etc. You could adapt McCloskey and Glucksberg's method to see whether the same principles hold for these categories. Note that, for abstract categories, you may need to restrict the exemplars to a particular category. For example, the abstract category *beautiful* could be related to cars, or buildings, or people.

Rosch's chapter is a rich source of ideas for further experiments in this area. You could investigate other measures of typicality (pp. 38–39), such as reaction time for categorising exemplars, rate of learning, and item output, and perhaps look at what the relationships are between these measures. Alternatively, you could explore the implications of her ideas on the vertical dimension of categories (p. 30), with superordinate, basic level, and subordinate categories. For example, do subjects list more attributes for basic level categories? What effect does context have on categorisation (pp. 42–3)?

You might like to investigate the role of structural factors in category decisions by using artificial categories with dot patterns, stick figures, or schematic faces as stimuli (Rosch, p. 37). This would allow you to explore the role of various category structures in categorisation.

Rosch's ideas have been applied to two further areas, namely, the categorisation of events and of people. She devoted the last section of her chapter (pp. 43–6) to discussing what units of events might be equivalent to basic level categories and how prototypical events may be conceptualised. You could follow her suggestions there for an alternative experiment.

Similarly, Cantor and Mischel (1979) suggested that the notions of prototypes and fuzzy sets could be applied to the categorisation of people. Their work provides many ideas for further experiments. For example, you could investigate what types of behaviour lead people to be labelled 'extraverted' or 'introverted' and whether these labels change depending on the context or occasion (pp. 11 and 34). You could explore Cantor and Mischel's 'taxonomies of persons' (p. 16), and follow their ideas for using card sorting to establish empirically the classifications of groups of people. Do subjects list more unique attributes for basic level categories in such taxonomies? A particularly interesting topic to investigate would be the role of categorisations of people in predicting expectancies about behaviour (pp. 26–7).

Finally, an interesting extension of typicality effects to chess-memory performance was carried out by Goldin (1978). She compared memory for typical and atypical positions in chess games, using recall, recognition, and reconstruction with cueing as memory measures in three separate experiments. She found that over a wide range of chess skills, subjects' memory was superior for typical positions. If you have access to some chess players, you could perhaps repeat one of her experiments. You could discuss her conclusions (p. 651) concerning possible mechanisms and features used in this task.

References

McCloskey, M. E., and Glucksberg, S. Natural categories: Well defined or fuzzy sets? *Memory & Cognition*, 1978, 6, 462-72.

Rosch, E. Principles of categorization. In E. Rosch and B. B. Lloyd (eds). *Cognition and Categorization*. Hillsdale, New Jersey: Lawrence Erlbaum Associates, 1978.

References for Alternatives

Cantor, N., and Mischel, W. Prototypes in person perception. In L. Berkowitz (ed.). *Advances in Experimental Social Psychology*, vol. 12. New York: Academic Press, 1979.

Goldin, S. Memory for the ordinary: Typicality effects in chess memory. *Journal of Experimental Psychology: Human Learning and Memory*, 1978, 4, 605-16.

V

Language
and
speech

Introduction

The study of language processing deserves an important place in any study of cognition. Many cognitive processing studies use linguistic or verbal stimuli, most use spoken instructions and many produce results which suggest the importance of linguistic variables. For example, remembering sentences is easier than remembering isolated words, and sentences are, of course, defined in terms of linguistic structural variables.

Apart from the role of linguistic materials and variables in other cognitive studies, there is a multitude of puzzling and interesting questions about language processing in its own right. These questions are largely about cognitive operations, and research in the area draws heavily on the findings and experimental techniques of other cognitive processing studies.

The main research questions about language processing can be grouped roughly into seven areas: speech perception, reading, sentence perception and processing, discourse analysis, meaning, language acquisition, and the relation of language and thought. These areas are discussed in many introductory books, including Greene (1972 and 1975), Clark and Clark (1977), Slobin (1971), Deese (1970) and, to some extent, Glass, Holyoak, and Santa (1979). Both in the cognitive psychology and the language section of your library you should also find some more advanced general psycholinguistic books such as Fodor, Bever, and Garrett (1974), and some more specialised books of readings such as Cooper and Walker (1979), or Kolers, Wrolstad, and Bouma (1979). You can find research reports on psycholinguistics in a wide range of psychology journals. The following brief description of each of the research areas listed above will set the scene for an outline of the workshops on language.

The areas of speech perception and of reading are concerned with the initial, especially perceptual, processing of language in its spoken and written forms respectively. Among the interesting findings here is the discovery that sounds which are heard as being the same are not necessarily acoustically identical. Psychological identity is not the same as physical identity. For example, the sound waves for the *d* sound in 'dog', 'daze', and 'deep' are all rather different. An intriguing puzzle to reading researchers concerns the role of the 'inner voice' so many of us hear when we read silently. Is this acoustic phenomenon an integral part of the reading process or an unnecessary by-product? Speech perception and reading tend to receive scant coverage in introductory texts, but they are mentioned by Clark and Clark (1977), Glass *et al.* (1979), and Deese (1970). Workshop L6 investigates some reading phenomena using a visual search task and workshop A2 in the attention area also has some implications for reading. Although not dealing with the speech-pattern recognition problems discussed above, one of the alternatives to L1 deals with how we listen to spoken language.

Sentence perception and processing concerns the way we comprehend and utter sentences, arguably the most important linguistic units we use daily. Many experiments here have investigated the importance of theories suggested by linguists such as Noam Chomsky (Greene, 1972 and 1975, and Slobin, 1971). Linguistic theories stress the distinction between what they call 'deep' and 'surface' structures and the importance of syntactic transformational rules. Some support for the psychological importance of these linguistic theories has been found. Workshops L1 and L2 both deal with sentence perception and processing, but using different experimental paradigms: the first uses a shadowing task whereas the second uses an immediate memory task. It is interesting to note that, as one of the alternatives to Workshop L2 suggests, not all current theories of sentence processing see the transformational linguistics which Chomsky introduced as having much to offer theories of sentence processing.

Some researchers prefer not to look at isolated sentences but concentrate on our processing of continuous discourse. Their main interest is often in the effects of context on language processing, in our treatment of ideas which can extend across sentence boundaries, and in how our language processing is affected by our knowledge of the world (Clark and Clark, 1977; Greene, 1972, 1975; Glass *et al.*, 1979; and Slobin, 1971). The role of extra-linguistic information on discourse processing is investigated using a memory task in Workshop L3. Workshop L7 also deals with discourse processing but concentrates on the internal structure of discourse and on the way people combine and organise information from several sentences. Alternatives to this workshop investigate language processing in two quite common situations for students: having a conversation, and reading part of a textbook and its summary.

The problems of meaning concern the representation and organisation of our semantic memories or of whatever passes for our mental 'dictionaries' (Clark and Clark, 1977; and Slobin, 1971). We can readily understand what others say, and can formulate our own ideas into words, so our mental dictionary must be a fairly flexible one. A worrying question here concerns the extent to which this dictionary is at all distinct from our knowledge of the world. If it is not distinct then this dictionary is even more complex than we may have thought. Workshops L4 and L5 look at problems of meaning and ambiguity. They both use reaction time measures, L4 with a word/non-word decision task and L5 with a sentence verification task.

Within the area of language acquisition we are, of course, interested in how people learn to use language (Clark and Clark, 1977; and Deese, 1970). We might ask questions about the order in which children acquire various grammatical rules, or we might try to find out what cognitive apparatus is necessary for language acquisition by teaching American Sign Language to chimpanzees.

The relation of language and thought is a thorny problem which has led to a great variety of research ranging from experiments on the thinking of deaf, language-deprived children to the language of thinking-deprived animals like chimpanzees. There are also some very interesting comparisons of the habitual cognitive and perceptual patterns of speakers of different languages. Greene (1975) and Clark and Clark (1977) both discuss these topics.

The language workshops cover several of the topic areas mentioned above and also illustrate a range of experimental methods. It was not possible to cover all the areas mentioned earlier. Language development was not included because courses in cognitive processes usually concentrate on adult behaviour. Additionally, speech perception, and the relation of language and thought were not included because experiments in these two areas tend to require specialised apparatus or materials. The workshops included allow some insight into the theoretical and experimental problems of the topic both for the students running the workshop and for those acting as subjects.

References

Clark, H. H., and Clark, E. V. *Psychology and Language: An Introduction to Psycholinguistics.* New York: Harcourt-Brace-Jovanovich, 1977.

Cooper, W. E., and Walker, E. C. T. *Sentence processing: Psycholinguistic Studies Presented to Merrill Garrett.* Hillsdale, New Jersey: Lawrence Erlbaum Associates, 1979.

Deese, J. *Psycholinguistics.* Boston: Allyn & Bacon, 1970.

Fodor, J. A., Bever, T. G., and Garrett, M. F. *The Psychology of Language: An Introduction to Psycholinguistics and Generative Grammar.* New York: McGraw-Hill, 1974.

Glass, A. L., Holyoak, K. J., and Santa, J. L. *Cognition.* Reading, Mass.: Addison-Wesley Publishing Co., 1979.

Greene, J. *Psycholinguistics: Chomsky and Psychology.* Harmondsworth, Middlesex: Penguin, 1972.

Greene, J. *Thinking and Language.* London: Methuen, 1975.

Kolers, P. A., Wrolstad, M. E., and Bouma, H. *Processing of Visible Language*, vol. 1. New York: Plenum Press, 1979.

Slobin, D. *Psycholinguistics*. Glenview, Illinois; Scott, Foresman, 1971.

L1 The birth of psycholinguistics

Do psychologists really need to listen to linguists?

Following Chomsky's revolutionary new linguistic theory towards the end of the 1950s and his strong denial of the prevailing stimulus-response view of language behaviour, optimism surged within the psychology of language. It was felt that an incorporation of Chomsky's linguistic rules into psycholinguistic theory would provide a ready and credible psychology of language processing. Greene (1975, ch. 6) provides a very readable resume of this historical background.

Among the first studies designed to test the above view was one by Miller and Isard (1963). This study aimed to show the importance of linguistic rules in language processing. Their finding was that sentences were better shadowed and, these authors argued, more intelligible the more the sentences obeyed such rules. Miller and Isard concluded that any theory of language processing 'must take into account the syntactic and semantic rules of the language' (Miller and Isard, p. 227). Perhaps this conclusion is unsurprising today, but it was in striking contrast to the stimulus-response views of its time, which tended to ignore the internal structures of sentences.

General procedure

This workshop will generally follow the procedures Miller and Isard used and it will be concerned with the same basic question whether linguistic rules need to be incorporated into psycholinguistics.

You will need a tape recording of several grammatical, anomalous, and ungrammatical sentences. Grammatical sentences obey both syntactic and semantic rules (e.g. 'The postman blew his whistle loudly'). Anomalous sentences follow the syntactic rules in having their nouns, verbs, etc., in the right places, but violate semantic rules (e.g. 'The barbecue signed her coffee furiously'). Ungrammatical strings violate both sorts of rules (e.g. 'Barbecue the his coffee blew postman'). The examples which Miller and Isard include in their Appendix may help you construct your sentences.

Subjects will listen to these sentences and shadow them. If time and scoring facilities permit, you could use individual testing, with subjects shadowing orally by repeating aloud what they hear. However, the experiment could be run in a group session if written shadowing were used. For this procedure, subjects would write down the sentences word by word as they heard them.

The presentation rate of the sentences will depend in part on the type of shadowing you use. How many sentences you use will depend on your available time, although you should use at least six of each type. Most subjects will need some shadowing practice, so you should allow time and some additional sentences for this.

You will probably use a repeated measures design, with all subjects shadowing all the types of sentences. In this case the sentences should be presented in a random order.

You will need to decide the best way to score the shadowing. You could record the number of complete sentences correctly shadowed, the number of words correctly shadowed, or the number of principal words correct. Miller and Isard use each of these methods, but you may decide to use yet another procedure.

In discussion, you might include consideration of the experiment's use of shadowing to tap language processing, and the experiment's consequent implications for theories of language processing. Is Miller and Isard's conclusion, quoted above, a reasonable one? Were subjects better able to shadow grammatical sentences? Do both syntactic and semantic rules have psychological reality?

Alternatives

Depending on available time and subjects, you could add a second factor to the experiment by having some examples of each type of sentence presented under each of several intensities of masking noise. Miller and Isard do this in their second experiment.

You might investigate the effects of instructions or experimental set, as do Miller and Isard in their third experiment. When subjects expect ungrammatical sentences can they shadow them more readily?

You could investigate whether the shadowing effect which Miller and Isard report is reflected in other measures of processing difficulty. For example, using a memory measure you could ask whether subjects better recall sentences which obey the linguistic rules.

Jarvella (1971) offers an interesting alternative which investigates the role of phrase structural constituents in processing passages. He asked subjects to listen to recordings of a passage with a view to answering subsequent comprehension questions on it. In addition he periodically stopped the recordings and asked subjects to recall verbatim as much of the immediately preceding passage as they could. He found that subjects recalled best any words from the clause in which the stoppage occurred, next best those from the preceding clause in the same sentence, and next words from a preceding sentence.

These results suggest that phrase structure constitutents play an important role in listening processes. Jarvella suggests that we maintain a verbatim memory only until we reach major constituent boundaries at which point the surface constituents are semantically interpreted and replaced by the next constituents. You could investigate this by replicating or extending Jarvella's research, perhaps concentrating on the cued recall technique of his Experiment 2, which controls for recall order effects. Instead of looking at verbatim memory you might consider a less restrictive scoring criterion of memory for meaning.

References

Greene, J. *Thinking and Language*. London: Methuen, 1975.
Miller, G., and Isard, S. Some perceptual consequences of linguistic rules. *Journal of Verbal Learning and Verbal Behavior*, 1963, 2, 217-28.

Reference for Alternatives

Jarvella, R. J. Syntactic processing of connected speech. *Journal of Verbal Learning and Verbal Behavior*, 1971, **10**, 409-16.

L2 Transformation rules

In listening to sentences do we actively use passive transformations?

By the early 1960s Noam Chomsky had established the need for trans-formation rules within linguistic theory. These transformation rules were rules like the passive and question transformations which allowed the for-mation of passive and question sentences, respectively, from simple 'kernel' sentences. For example, applying the passive transformation to a kernel like 'The dog bit the postman' would lead to the passive sentence 'The post-man was bitten by the dog'. If you are not familiar with transformational linguistic theory you should consult an introductory psycholinguistic text such as Clark and Clark (1977, ch. 1, especially pp. 10–24) for a fuller dis-cussion of this linguistic background when preparing for this workshop.

During the 1960s several psycholinguistic researchers produced evidence for the transformationalist view that specific linguistic transformations were somehow embodied in our cognitive processes. The idea was that the linguists' rules paralleled the operations in our heads. For example, we understand a passive sentence like 'The postman was bitten by the dog' only by undoing the passive transformation and deriving its kernel sentence.

Savin and Perchonock (1965) suggested that sentences were represented in memory as simple kernel sentences tagged with transformation tags. By reapplying the tagged transformations to the kernel the original sentence could be reproduced and recalled. These transformation tags would form additional 'chunks' in short-term memory (STM). Savin and Perchonock argued that the more transformationally complex a sentence is, the more transformations have to be applied to derive it from its kernel. So, for ex-ample, the sentence 'Who was bitten by the dog?' involves a passive and a question transformation, while only passive transformation is involved in 'The postman was bitten by the dog'. Remembering transformationally more complex sentences would involve our storing additional transfor-mation tags in STM and would therefore require more chunks in STM. Therefore less spare STM capacity would remain for remembering other material.

This workshop is based on Savin and Perchonock's experiment. Their experiment is fascinating because of their attempt to measure this spare STM capacity. They asked subjects to remember a sentence and some additional words. Their findings supported the transformationalist view. Fewer additional words were recalled with transformationally more complex sentences, thus suggesting the presence of extra transformational tags in STM for these complex sentences.

General procedure

You will need a tape recording of the sentences, each followed by its additional words to be recalled. Allow an interval between sentences for the recall tasks. You might use cueing tones to indicate when sentences or word lists are to begin.

It is probably sufficient to use just three or four transformational sentence types (e.g. kernels, passives, questions, and passive questions). You should have at least five examples of each sentence type. Try to ensure that the sentence length is not confounded with transformational complexity, although this may be difficult, as Savin and Perchonock themselves had difficulty on this point. For the additional words, you could use randomly selected lists or category lists such as Savin and Perchonock used.

You should instruct subjects about the format of your tape recording and tell them that their main task is to recall a series of sentences presented one at a time. Once they have recalled the sentence for a trial they should also try to recall as many as they can of the additional words presented after the sentence. You should stress that verbatim recall of the sentences is their primary task. Some practice trials would be a good idea.

Score the number of additional words correctly recalled for each correctly recalled sentence. It is probably best to omit data where sentences are not correctly recalled. Average across subjects and sentences to produce the mean number of additional words recalled for each sentence type. Do transformationally more complex sentences lead to reduced recall of additional words?

In discussion, you might consider how the results bear on the transformationalist view, especially in the light of the interesting methodology of this experiment. One fascinating methodological problem concerns just how we interpret this experiment now that the theory of a fixed capacity STM 'box' has fallen from favour. Another problem concerns the control of sentence length as a confounding variable. A more difficult problem concerns the interpretation of experiments such as Savin and Perchonock's in the light of more recent and much revised transformational linguistics.

Alternatives

Your linguistic expertise and your available testing time will determine which and how many transformational sentence types you investigate.

As an addition to the experiment, you could control sentence length more carefully than did Savin and Perchonock. You might, for example, use a range of sentence lengths and correlate the average number of extra words recalled with sentence length, ignoring transformational complexity. A strong negative correlation would support the view that the important factor was sentence length.

Alternatively you could control for the factor Perfetti (1969) called 'lexical density'. This is a measure of the relative amount of semantic content in sentences of equal length and it is computed by finding the ratio of content words to non-content words like 'and' and 'the'. Perfetti argued that this semantic factor is a better predictor of memory performance than are the syntactic factors first introduced by Chomsky.

James and Abrahamson (1977) discussed several ways in which the encoding of active and passive sentences might differ. They suggested that differences for active and passive sentences may result from 'reconstructive biases' in recall. Using recognition tests they found no differences in memory for active and passive sentences, contrary to Savin and Perchonock. You could try to replicate their experiment or you might extend their study by looking at transformations other than the passive.

Clark and Clark (ch. 2) offered a wide range of suggestions about processing strategies used in sentence comprehension. These suggestions did not involve transformations. You could follow up this discussion by trying to find further evidence about our use of such processing strategies. This might involve a recall or recognition paradigm but it need not do so.

References

Clark, H. H., and Clark, E. V. *Psychology and Language: An Introduction to Psycholinguistics*. New York:Harcourt, Brace, Jovanovich, 1977, (chs 1 and 2).

Savin, H., and Perchonock, E. Grammatical structure and immediate recall of English sentences. *Journal of Verbal Learning and Verbal Behavior*, 1965, **4**, 348–53.

References for Alternatives

James, C. T., and Abrahamson, A. A. Recognition memory for active and passive sentences. *Journal of Psycholinguistic Research*, 1977, **6**, 37–47.

Perfetti, C. A. Lexical density and phrase structure depth as variables in sentence retention. *Journal of Verbal Learning and Verbal Behavior*, 1969, **8**, 719–24.

L3 Extra-linguistic context

How much more do we hear than is actually said?

Many researchers feel that experiments looking at processing of isolated words or sentences are unrealistic and do not tell us how we process language in everyday life, when, for example, we engage in conversations or listen to the radio. Some of these researchers have tried to tap real-life language processing by using prose passages as stimuli. These prose experiments tend to investigate global linguistic variables such as comprehension, understanding, and memory for content rather than for verbatim form. Indeed our first workshop, 'Introduction to cognition', showed how providing an otherwise incomprehensible passage with a suitable context not only made the passage comprehensible, but also lead to better recall of the ideas in the passage than when the context was not provided.

This workshop will differ by using readily comprehensible passages and asks whether changing the supposed identity of the author affects the memory of the passages. Wertsch (1975), for example, proposed that people's understanding of a passage can be influenced by their beliefs about the speaker's identity. This suggests that a listener's understanding is not simply a matter of linguistic expertise but also of knowledge of the world. Hasher and Griffin (1978) suggested that these knowledge of the world factors mainly operate at the time of retrieval. In this workshop we are interested in the degree to which extra-linguistic information affects our memory for prose and whether the locus of any effect of such information is largely at storage or at retrieval.

General procedure

We can investigate these questions by using an approach from Hasher and Griffin, or Wertsch, or a combination of both. If you use Hasher and Griffin's procedure you might follow their example and take care to appear especially disorganised in running the experiment! You will need a prose passage which is readily comprehensible but which is vague enough to be reasonably attributed to different sources or themes. These sources might be individuals, organisations, or types of individuals. You will need to devise a passage using comments made in the references as a guide. You might present the passages in either written or spoken form, keeping in mind that if you present it in spoken form you should not allow intonation to bias the passage.

Two or, if numbers permit, several groups can be used. These experimental groups could be distinguished by (1) the supposed source or theme, or (2) whether the theme or source is changed after hearing the passage, or (3) some other factor you decide upon. You could prepare separate sets of written instructions and test all the groups together, or you might locate the groups in separate rooms. Pilot testing of passages, recognition sentences and/or rating of idea units will probably be necessary.

For a response measure, you could adopt Wertsch's method (p. 91) using recognition sentences and score false recognitions of the various kinds. On the other hand you could follow Hasher and Griffin and use idea recall. Alternatively, you might use some combination of these procedures. When the experiment is complete, subjects can score one another's response protocols.

In discussion, you might consider the implications of your findings for language processing theories. How widespread a phenomenon is extra-linguistic determination of meaning in our everyday lives? To what extent can psycholinguistic theories deal with language independently of the uses to which it is put and the contexts in which it occurs? What do you think of Hasher and Griffin's theoretical model involving reproductive and reconstructive processes in recall? You should also consider what your results and others in the literature suggest about encoding versus retrieval explanations of context effects.

Alternatives

There are already several places in the main workshop where you have to decide between different procedures. For example, you could follow Hasher and Griffin's general method but use Wertsch's recognition procedure to test memory. Alternatively, you could test Hasher and Griffin's claim that the effects of extra-linguistic factors can be lessened by emphasising the importance of recall accuracy to subjects prior to presentation of the prose material.

Anderson and Pichert (1978) have conducted an experiment similar to Hasher and Griffin's. In their experiment subjects read a story either from the perspective of a home-buyer or from the perspective of a burglar. Following initial recall, subjects were asked to recall the story again but using the alternative perspective as an aid. It was found that more information pertinent to the changed perspective was remembered on the second recall attempt. This finding may appear contrary to that of Hasher and Griffin. Although both sets of experimenters argue for retrieval-based effects of schemata in story recall, they differ in their interpretation of how these schemata operate. Hasher and Griffin suggested a second theme produces more accurate (reproductive) recall while Anderson and Pichert suggested a second theme produces a different (reconstructive) recall. However, not only procedures but also the measures used to assess the experimental effects are different between the two experiments. Hasher and Griffin used theme-related intrusions and idea accuracy as their measures, whereas Anderson and Pichert used theme relevant ideas. It would be interesting to assess whether the two sets of data are really in conflict by (a) controlling the procedural differences and (b) using all three measures to examine story recall.

Owens, Bower and Black (1979) used a different technique to study the effects of extra-linguistic knowledge on story recall. Prior to receiving a neutral story subjects were provided with an ambiguous three-line description of the main characters' motives. Owens *et al.* argued that our interpretation of these descriptions serve as a schema and influence our understanding of otherwise neutral elements in the story. Both recognition and recall tests demonstrated such an effect. You could either replicate Owens *et al.*'s experiment or you could re-run the study incorporating some of the procedural and or measurement techniques noted.

References

Wertsch, J. V. The influence of listener perception of the speaker on recognition memory. *Journal of Psycholinguistic Research*, 1975, **4**, 89–98.

Hasher, L., and Griffin, G. Reconstructive and reproductive processes in memory. *Journal of Experimental Psychology: Human Learning and Memory*, 1978, **4**, 318–30.

References for Alternatives

Anderson, R. C., and Pichert, J. W. Recall of previously unrecallable information following a shift in perspective. *Journal of Verbal Learning and Verbal Behavior*, 1978, **17**, 1–12.

Owens, J., Bower, G. H., and Black, J. B. The 'soap opera' effect in story recall. *Memory & Cognition*, 1979, **7**, 185–91.

L4 Lexical search

How do we look up words in our heads?

To understand all the words we do, we must have some record of them in our heads, some sort of mental dictionary or lexicon. In trying to provide a theory of this lexicon, one question which arises concerns words with several meanings. Do such words have just one entry in the mental lexicon or several distinct entries, perhaps one for each meaning? This problem is fairly obvious for recognised ambiguous words like 'bank', but it may be a more widespread problem, if, as Barclay, Bransford, Franks, McCarrell and Nitsch (1974) argue, most common words are to some extent ambiguous.

If some words do have multiple entries in our mental lexicons, then these lexicons must be organised rather differently from dictionaries. Perhaps our mental lexicons are indexed by meanings rather than by initial letters as in printed dictionaries. Perhaps we can mentally look up meanings or topic areas much as we would look up a thesaurus or an encyclopaedia. Such access via meanings could have important implications for other theories of language processing (e.g. the theories of how context influences sentence processing).

This workshop will follow an experiment designed by Jastrzembski and Stanners (1975, Experiment 1) to see whether ambiguous words do have several entries in our mental lexicons. These authors argue that if ambiguous words have several entries, then they should on average be found more quickly than other words during a search through the mental lexicon.

To test this view Jastrzembski and Stanners used a lexical search, or word recognition, task in which subjects were asked to judge, as quickly as possible, whether a given string of letters was an English word. Some strings were words, while others were non-words which can be more or less like English (e.g. 'hiuse' or 'brwafr'). The main response variable was the subject's reaction time in making the judgment. Jastrzembski and Stanners implicitly assumed that the task requires subjects to search through their mental lexicons much as we would search through a book, and to respond positively only when they found the word presented. Such searches should be quicker, on the average, for words with several entries in the lexicon.

General procedure

For this workshop you will need two lists of common words. One list of ambiguous words will have a high number of meanings (HNM), while words in the other list will have a low number of meanings (LNM). Jastrzembski and Stanners's HNM words averaged about thirty-five meanings each, while their LNM words averaged only about eight. You may not be able to compose such extreme lists, but you should ensure that the lists are clearly distinct. Working out these lists will probably require some fairly lengthy consultation with a large unabridged dictionary. Be careful that word frequency (i.e. frequency of usage) does not differ markedly between the lists. You might also control for variables like word length and initial letter by matching words across lists.

In addition to these experimental lists you will need two corresponding lists of non-words, and some practice items. You might follow Jastrzembski and Stanners and form each of the non-words by changing a single vowel in its corresponding HNM and LNM word, or you could use some more random procedure.

The practice items should include about half words and half non-words and should be roughly comparable to the experimental items. The actual number of practice and experimental items you use will depend in part on the time you have for testing. However you will need lists of at least five HNM and five LNM words.

You could present the stimuli using either a slide projector or a tachistoscope, and you will therefore have to prepare a photographic slide or a tachistoscope card for each item. You will need a timer attached to your projector or tachistoscope so that you can accurately measure subjects' reaction times from stimulus onset. On each trial your timer should start with stimulus onset and end as the subject indicates his word or non-word judgment.

A repeated measures design is probably most suitable here. Once subjects have been instructed about their task they will all see the same practice items and will all see both the HNM and LNM lists. The experimental words and non-words will be randomly ordered, and you could use a different random order for each subject or testing group.

If your reaction time equipment permits, you could test subjects in small groups. This would rule out using a tachistoscope but it would speed up testing and might allow you to use more stimuli.

The crucial reaction times are those for trials on which subjects correctly judge an HNM or an LNM word to be a word. Following Jastrzembski and Stanners, you can ignore the reaction times for error (i.e. 'non-word') responses to HNM or LNM words. However, if the number of these errors is very different for the two types of words then you may have to modify your overall conclusions.

While avoiding the complex data manipulations carried out by Jastrzembski and Stanners, it would be well to take some account of the usual skewness of reaction time data, of the repeated measures design, and of data missing because of omitted error responses. A relatively simply procedure would be to calculate for each subject his median correct reaction time for HNM words and that for LNM words. Then, for each list of words, calculate the means of these subject medians. You can then compare these average HNM and LNM scores to see whether they differ, as predicted by Jastrzembski and Stanners. Of course, if you do a significance test on these means it will have to be for dependent or related groups.

In discussion, you could consider what your results suggest about mental lexicons. More generally, you might consider the usefulness of the lexical search task itself. Is a mental search sufficiently like searching through a book for Jastrzembski and Stanners's experiment to tell us something about our mental lexicons? You could consider the problem of dealing with error reaction times. Should we just ignore them? What implications do the proposals of Barclay *et al*. have for the organisation of the lexicon?

Alternatives

With the right facilities, you could run the experiment on a small computer which has a cathode ray display screen. Once programmed, the computer could display stimuli as you desire and could record reaction times, perhaps from several subjects at once.

Following Jastrzembski and Stanners's approach (see their Table 1), you might want to use three or more levels of the number of meanings variable. This would allow correlation of reaction time and number of meanings. Control of word frequency would be especially important for this alternative.

If we do look up words in a mental lexicon, then it would need to be accessed in identifying and comprehending spoken as well as written words. You could see if Jastrzembski and Stanners's findings with visual materials can be replicated with aural presentations of words and non-words. Of course, your non-words would all have to be pronounceable and not homophonic with real words. You might also have to keep all items about the same length so that you could validly begin reaction timing from the beginning of each item.

Taft and Forster (1975) suggest that the lexicon includes not only words but also stem morphemes, like 'semble', from which words are constructed, e.g. 'assemble', 'resemble'. They found that it takes longer to decide that such non-words are not words than it takes to categorise other non-words. Because Jastrzembski and Stanners are primarily interested in word reaction times while Taft and Forster concentrate on non-word reaction times, you could combine both these approaches into one experiment. You would have to ensure reasonable comparability of words and non-words.

The Barclay *et al*. experiment could make an interesting alternative, especially if you want to avoid reaction timing and tachistoscopic stimulus presentation. You could test the generality of their claims for semantic 'flexibility' of words normally considered unambiguous by using some different words and sentences in your study. As Barclay *et al.* suggest (p. 478), pilot work will be important when constructing your materials.

A more complicated experiment, in terms of materials, apparatus, and design, is the lexical search experiment by Schvaneveldt, Meyer, and Becker (1976). Rather than just looking at whether ambiguous words have multiple entries in our mental lexicons, these authors use context effects to see whether several meanings or just one meaning is mentally accessed each time we encounter such words. With a small group of students to work on it, such an experiment could provide a challenging and exciting workshop.

References

Barclay, J. R., Bransford, J. D., Franks, J. J., McCarrell, N. S., and Nitsch, K. Comprehension and semantic flexibility. *Journal of Verbal Learning and Verbal Behavior*, 1974, **13**, 471–81.

Jastrzembski, J. E., and Stanners, R. F. Multiple word meanings and lexical search speed. *Journal of Verbal Learning and Verbal Behavior*, 1975, **14**, 534–7.

References for Alternatives

Schvaneveldt, R. W., Meyer, D. E., and Becker, C. A. Lexical ambiguity, semantic context, and visual word recognition. *Journal of Experimental Psychology: Human Perception and Performance*, 1976, **2**, 243–56.

Taft, M., and Forster, K. I. Lexical storage and retrieval of prefixed words. *Journal of Verbal Learning and Verbal Behavior*, 1975, **14**, 638–47.

L5 Sentence ambiguity

How many meanings do we have in mind at once?

If, to borrow an example from MacKay (1966), I say, 'The witness was lying when the lawyer entered', then you probably understand that the witness was doing so through his teeth rather than on his back. Indeed, the ambiguity of my statement may not even have occurred to you. On the other hand you will easily recognise the intended ambiguity of puns such as Arthur Calwell's racist jibe that two Wongs don't make a white. Why do we sometimes readily appreciate ambiguity and at other times just fail to notice it?

Ambiguous sentences pose an interesting problem for any language-processing theory. While listening to ambiguous sentences do we, for example, keep all possible meanings in mind or just one meaning? We might keep all possible meanings in mind and only later decide which is the most likely in the context concerned. On the other hand, we might access just one meaning, perhaps that suggested by the prior context, and become aware of the ambiguity and alternative meanings only if we later seem mistaken about the sentence's meaning.

These questions have wider scope than you might initially imagine, since many everyday sentences are, strictly speaking, ambiguous. For example, 'He chased the cat with an injured leg' is ambiguous with respect to who was injured. Understanding how we comprehend ambiguous sentences should improve our general understanding of sentence processing.

This workshop will follow Foss, Bever and Silver (1968) in using a sentence verification task to investigate our processing of ambiguous sentences. For this task subjects must say as quickly as possible whether a picture they are shown correctly represents the sentence they just heard.

Foss, Bever and Silver argue that if subjects interpret an ambiguous sentence ambiguously (i.e. they have two meanings in mind at once), then their reaction times will be unaffected by which interpretation of the sentence is depicted in the picture. However, if subjects interpret the sentence in just one way, then their reaction times should be slower when the picture depicts the more unexpected interpretation of the sentence. This is because, when confronted with the unexpected picture, most subjects, who, by definition, will have interpreted the sentence in the expected way, will have to re-process the sentence before correctly responding that the picture does represent the sentence.

General procedure

To run the workshop you will need at least twelve ambiguous sentences. Use only lexical ambiguities, as they tend to produce the strongest results (Foss, Bever and Silver) and they do not require the special linguistic knowledge involved in analysing deep and surface structure ambiguities. You might get some ideas for your sentences from those listed by MacKay.

For each ambiguous sentence you will need two pictures or drawings, one depicting each of the sentence's meanings. To control for picture processing time you should ensure that all the pictures are comparable in complexity and difficulty, or at least that the pair of pictures for each sentence are comparable.

Some pre-testing will be needed to decide for each ambiguous sentence which is its expected meaning and picture. In choosing sentences you probably should use only sentences for which the expected meaning is clearly discernible.

To prevent subjects becoming unusually sensitive to ambiguity and consequently applying some abnormal sentence processing, you will need about twenty non-ambiguous filler sentences. Each of these filler sentences will have a corresponding picture, although in some cases these pictures will be 'wrong'. Wrong pictures will misrepresent their sentences by depicting the wrong subject, object or verb. For example, the picture for 'The dog chased the cat' could wrongly depict the dog chasing a postman. If you decide to have about half of the pictures right and about half wrong, then more than half of these filler sentences will have to be accompanied by wrong pictures. This control is introduced because the ambiguous sentences are all accompanied by right pictures.

Because you can present subjects with each sentence only once, you should use two groups of subjects. One group will get half of the ambiguous sentences with their expected pictures, and the other half with their unexpected pictures. For the second group, these pairings will be reversed. For both groups, the sentences should be randomly ordered and embedded in the same filler items. You might present several filler items first as practice items.

The sentences can be read aloud by the experimenter or presented from a tape recorder. Following each sentence you will present its picture, using a slide or an overhead projector, or a tachistoscope, or perhaps by turning over cards in front of the subject. Whichever way you present the pictures you will need an accurate measure from the picture onset until the subject responds 'right' or 'wrong'. If your reaction time equipment permits group testing, this would facilitate running the experiment.

We are primarily interested in how long it takes subjects correctly to respond 'right' for the expected and unexpected pictures associated with the ambiguous sentences. For each ambiguous sentence you can calculate the median of subjects' correct reaction times. Do this separately for each sentence's expected and unexpected pictures. Averaging these medians within expected and within unexpected pictures allows you to check for any overall difference in reaction time to expected and unexpected pictures.

It is probably best to ignore reaction times for trials on which subjects incorrectly respond 'wrong' to an ambiguous sentence's picture. However, if there are many such error responses, or if they are mostly for unexpected pictures, they may affect your final conclusions.

Foss, Bever and Silver say that their results are only tentative because they used few ambiguous sentences. Which model of sentence processing do your results support? In discussion you might also consider the argument that we need to look at the processing difficulty of ambiguous sentences not at the end of the sentence but during the processing itself. You might also discuss the problem of dealing with error reaction times. Reaction time experiments assume that particular internal processes are necessary to deal with the set task, but these processes probably do not occur for error responses.

Alternatives

If your expertise and facilities permit, you could investigate surface and deep structural ambiguities as well as lexical ambiguities. In addition, rather than following Foss, Bever, and Silver's sentence verification technique, you could use MacKay's sentence completion task.

You might follow Holmes (1979) in looking at how context affects the processing of ambiguous sentences. This additional variable could be added to the picture verification task by using some well-chosen sentence contexts prior to the critical sentences (see Holmes's Experiment 5) in order more carefully to control which is the expected and which is the unexpected sentence meaning.

Holmes also claims that possible meanings of a lexical ambiguity are accessed one at a time with the most frequent, or most common, meaning accessed first, except for some percentage of the times when there is a preceding biasing context. This stress on the importance of the relative commonness of the possible meanings is an interesting new theoretical development in the area. You could check this theory by extending her experiments, using either her semantic anomaly or her ambiguity detection tasks. You might also use these tasks in some different experiments of your own.

References

Foss, D. J., Bever, T. G., and Silver, M. The comprehension and verification

of ambiguous sentences. *Perception & Psychophysics*, 1968, **4**, 304–6.
MacKay, D. G. To end ambiguous sentences. *Perception & Psychophysics*, 1966, **1**, 426–36.

Reference for Alternatives

Holmes, V. M. Accessing ambiguous words during sentence comprehension. *Quarterly Journal of Experimental Psychology*, 1979, **31**, 569–89.

L6 Reading units

Do we read letters?

As Bradshaw (1975) points out, an interesting problem in our study of the reading process concerns the units by which we read. Do we read letter by letter, or by some larger units such as syllables, words, or perhaps even sentences? This question is a difficult but important one. For instance, only if letters are the units by which we usually read can we expect the volumes of theory and research on single-letter perception to be generally helpful to our understanding of reading. Additionally, what the usual and optimal reading units are may have some bearing on the teaching of reading, and on speed reading, and its training.

For investigating reading units, Healey (1976) offers a technique involving an interesting variant of the visual search paradigm. Healey asked subjects to read a passage and simultaneously to note all occurrences of the letter t in the passage. She argues that this enables us to check whether people do read letter by letter or whether some t's are overlooked because they are part of some larger reading unit, such as the common word 'the'. Because her instructions emphasised reading, she also claims that her technique is better than many others such as the tachistoscopic ones which Bradshaw discusses. Healey suggests that these other tasks do not really involve reading and that they may well involve processes which are very different from reading processes.

General procedure

This workshop will be based on Healey's first experiment. In this experiment Healey was trying to show that common words like *the* are read as units and that their letters are not read separately and are therefore not well detected. You will need one or more prose passages which subjects read, circling occurrences of the target letter t as they go. Several of these t's should occur in the common word context *the*. In addition you will need a scrambled-letter passage, constructed by using the same passage with the punctuation, spacing, and target t's in the same locations, but with all the other letters randomly scrambled. To ensure a useful analysis of results, each passage should have at least six t's in '*the*' locations and six in the other locations. 'A *t* in a *the* location occurs in the word *the* in the prose passage or in the corresponding location in the scrambled-letter passage' (Healey, p. 236).

You should counterbalance the presentation orders of the passages you use. Some subjects will read a prose passage first and others will 'read' a scrambled one first. Your instructions should follow Healey's in stressing reading rather than letter search. This could involve an emphasis on maintaining normal reading speed in spite of missing some target letters. Of course this may not be easy for the scrambled letter passage. Subjects can use stopwatches to time themselves on each passage.

Record, for each subject, the time taken to read each passage and the number of target letters missed in *the* locations and in other locations within each passage. Calculate for each passage, and compare across passages the average reading time, the average number of targets missed, and the percentage of the total number of missed targets which occur in *the* locations. Healey found that this conditional percentage of errors was the most sensitive measure to use. It can be compared to the chance percentage of missed targets occurring in *the* locations. This chance percentage is simply the percentage of targets in *the* locations. Are more targets missed in *the* locations than would be expected by chance? Are more targets in *the* locations missed in the original passage than in the scrambled-letter passage?

In discussion, you could consider how well Healey's search-like task involves and exposes our reading processes. What do your results suggest about the units we use in reading? What other evidence can you think of which suggests that we do not read letter by letter? Discussion might also include a consideration of Healey's arguments concerning the speed/accuracy trade-off that she found. Did you find such a trade-off? Does Healey's unitisation hypothesis explain her results and yours better than the other hypotheses she discusses?

Alternatives

Instead of using *t* as the target letter and *the* as the common word context, you could use a different target letter and/or a different common word context, as Drewnowski and Healey (1980) did.

You might also check that subjects are really reading the passages and not just doing the search task. Perhaps you could give some comprehension questions following the prose passage to test for memory of its content. Of course this will not be possible for scrambled passages.

You might include in your passage several different common words to see whether letter detection is generally depressed in common words (Healey, Experiment 4). By inserting some rare words you could investigate whether letter detection was enhanced within that sort of word. As mentioned, you should ensure that there are sufficient examples of whatever types of word contexts you use to allow a meaningful analysis of the results.

In addition to the prose and scrambled-letter passages mentioned above. Healey's methodology could be applied to other types of passages, including 'scrambled-word' passages (Healey, Experiment 2) and list passages (Drewnowski, 1978). As Drewnowski (1978) and Drewnowski and Healey (1980) argue, experiments with different stimulus passages can highlight use of different reading units. It seems that we can read in letter, morpheme, word, or phrase units at different times. You will have to decide how many passages you can use and which ones best investigate the questions which most interest you.

If you have access to some beginning readers it would be interesting to see whether, as Drewnowski claims, they tend to use smaller reading units more often than skilled readers do. Reference to Drewnowski's results could suggest appropriate reading ages to investigate.

References

Bradshaw, J. Three interrelated problems in reading: A review. *Memory & Cognition*, 1975, **3**, 123-34.

Healey, A. F. Detection errors on the word *the*: Evidence for reading units larger than letters. *Journal of Experimental Psychology: Human Perception and Performance*, 1976, **2**, 235-42.

References for Alternatives

Drewnowski, A. Detection errors on the word *the*: Evidence for the acquisition of reading levels. *Memory & Cognition*, 1978, **6**, 403-9.

Drewnowski, A., and Healey, A. F. Missing *-ing* in reading: Letter detection errors on word endings. *Journal of Verbal Learning and Verbal Behavior*, 1980, **19**, 247-62.

L7 Understanding discourse
Do you use your own script when you read a story?

Although a great deal of psycholinguistic research is concerned with how we process single words or single sentences, our everyday use of language includes conversations, and reading or listening to narratives and to more theoretical nonfiction accounts of the world (such as you are reading now!). Understanding such connected discourse involves not only factors controlling word and sentence comprehension, but also additional factors which come into play only when series of sentences need to be combined for understanding. These additional factors are concerned with how we combine information from different sentences, with the logical or the narrative structure in passages, and with the cognitive structures resulting from our encoding of passages.

In addition, our processing of discourse is likely to reflect the organisation of our general knowledge of the world because it is often this knowledge which allows us to expand upon and to understand fully what we hear and read. For example, if I say 'I ate in a restaurant last night and I tipped the waiter', it is your knowledge about restaurants and eating out which allows you to understand me properly. You do not need to have been discussing a particular waiter or to assume that the restaurant has only one waiter to understand the reference of 'the waiter'.

It has been suggested (e.g. Black and Bower, 1979; Graesser, Woll, Kowalski, and Smith, 1980) that this sort of world knowledge may be embodied in 'scripts' we have in mind for many conventional activities like eating out at a restaurant, getting up in the morning, going to the doctor, and changing a flat tyre. A script is a cognitive organisation which includes a sequence of the main goal-directed actions and roles involved in a conventional activity. For example, the script for going to the doctor would involve a main goal (to be cured), roles of doctor, patient, and perhaps receptionist, and actions like making an appointment, going to the surgery, sitting in the waiting room, perhaps skimming the inevitable old magazines, seeing the doctor, and so on. Aspects of a script can be more or less typical of the script. Consider, for example, the script for going to the doctor. Visiting the surgery is probably very typical in these days when doctors are reluctant to make house calls. Making an appointment is probably less typical in that it is not always necessary. Other events like finding a wallet left in the waiting room are probably atypical since they are possible but are probably not part of some general script for going to the doctor.

Graesser *et al.* suggested that when we listen to or read a narrative we encode it in terms of such scripts and that these facilitate our processing by providing ready-made frameworks onto which we can fit the various episodes in a narrative. Once the topic 'going to the doctor' is mentioned we can access our script for this activity and use this script to guide our inferences, to provide ready-made roles for the characters, and to provide an implicit rationale for many actions mentioned.

Although less clearly in favour of script theory, Black and Bower acknowledged that their data are consistent with this approach. They agreed that stories are encoded in terms of 'episodes' (which are similar to Graesser *et al.*'s scripted activities). Moreover, they produced evidence that each episode in a story forms a separate chunk in memory.

Graesser *et al.* also looked at memory performance for some firm evidence that scripts are used in our processing of discourse. They suggested that encoding in terms of scripts leads to better memory. Specifically they proposed that the language comprehender accesses a script as soon as the relevant topic is mentioned and forms a memory trace for each scripted activity (e.g. going to the doctor) that occurs. Each of these memory traces contains a script pointer indicating the relevant script and separate tags for any actions or events which are atypical for that script (e.g. finding a wallet in the doctor's waiting room). In general, their results supported this proposal. For example, recognition memory for events mentioned in a story was better for atypical than for typical events in a script. This had been predicted because atypical events are separately tagged in memory, while typical events which did and did not occur would be confused since they are all encoded in the one script pointer.

This workshop will be based on Graesser *et al.*'s work. It will examine memory performance to see whether scripts are involved in discourse processing and to test their 'script pointer + tag' hypothesis. In particular the workshop will compare recognition and/or recall for typical and atypical events of conventional (or scripted) activities mentioned in a story.

General procedure

You will need a story involving several short episodes, or scripted activities, such as waking up, travelling to university, going to a class, and having lunch at a cafeteria. You could use Graesser *et al.* and Black and Bower as guides to construct such a story, perhaps beginning with a section from a novel. Each episode in your story should include several actions, some typical and others atypical. Some pilot work will help determine exactly how many episodes and actions per episode to use, keeping in mind possible ceiling and floor effects. You could be largely guided by your own intuitions about which actions are typical and which are atypical for each episode because there is generally high agreement among people about the typicality of actions for conventional activities. Nevertheless, it might be a good idea to ask three or four people to rate the actions in each episode for typicality. If you use a recognition memory test, then these ratings can be used to guide the construction of confusion items which match the memory items in typicality. Following Graesser *et al.*, you could either divide your actions into several typicality levels (their Experiment 1) or simply classify them as typical and atypical as in their Experiment 2.

Ask subjects to listen to the passage or to read it once, telling them that they will later be asked questions about the story. Graesser *et al.* used three different memory tests: recall, yes/no recognition, and two-alternative forced-choice (2AFC) recognition. You could use any of these tests with different subjects for each test. For example, you could use two groups if you wanted to compare recognition and recall. Such a comparison could be interesting since Graesser *et al.* predicted and found different results for these two tests, especially after a few days' delay. Since they reported no marked differences between yes/no and 2AFC recognition, you could choose whichever of these you preferred. The number of memory tests you use will depend on your interests and available resources.

Recognition memory tests would need to include the actions mentioned in each episode and an equal number of distractor actions not mentioned but matched for typicality with those mentioned. Following Graesser *et al.* you might decide to block the actions for each episode under a cueing heading for that episode. For a recall test simply ask subjects to write down as much as they can from the story. Alternatively, you could use Graesser *et al.*'s procedure which involved providing a heading for each episode as a cue for recall.

You will need to decide what retention interval to use between subjects' reading the passage and having a memory test of it. Keeping in mind Graesser *et al.*'s findings and your testing arrangements should allow you to decide this point. If your retention interval is relatively short, then you could fill it with some other task, unrelated to the passage.

For a 2AFC recognition test you can simply score the number correct, separately for typical and atypical actions. For a yes/no recognition test you would need to score both correct recognitions and false alarms separately for each level of typicality. A recall test would require you to count the number of items recalled for each typicality level and also assign any intrusions to the appropriate typicality level. As Graesser *et al.* showed, scoring both recall intrusion and yes/no recognition false alarms is crucial in detecting all of the memory effects of scripts. Note that verbatim recall is not essential.

If your statistical expertise extends to signal detection analysis, you could calculate d' for the recognition tests. In addition, Graesser *et al.*'s Memory Improvement score would provide a single score combining correct and intrusion recall scores. Does memory performance depend on typicality level?

In discussion you should consider whether your results support the script pointer + tag theory which Graesser *et al.* defended. Did you find different results for recall and recognition? You could also ask your subjects whether they were aware of using scripts in comprehending the passage. Is it likely that we use scripts in comprehension of non-narrative prose passages? What about in other situations or tasks?

Alternatives

As mentioned above, Black and Bower (1979) found evidence that story texts are encoded in terms of episodes for which we have scripts and that these episodes form chunks in short-term memory. You might see whether you, too, can find evidence supporting this. Perhaps you could try more than two episodes in each story.

Graesser *et al.*'s results, however, suggest that some additional controls may be required in Black and Bower's experiment, for example, controlling for typicality. Black and Bower's manipulation of episode length involved simply adding actions to each episode but these actions had not been previously rated for typicality. Their importance ratings (Experiment 2) are not really typicality ratings and in any case they did not systematically investigate memory for items of high and low importance. Graesser *et al.*'s results suggest that additional actions which are typical may be encoded in the script chunk but that atypical additional actions may form an additional tag (chunk?) in memory. Just as controlling for the typicality of additional actions in an episode is likely to be important, it may also be important to equate the typicality of any recognition test distractors.

In addition, Grasser *et al.* showed that we must consider not only percentage of correct recall and recognition but also recall intrusions and recognition false alarms. Black and Bower did not do this, which may explain why they reported better recall for their target (typical?) actions than for their filler actions, while Graesser *et al.* found that when recall was corrected for guessing, memory was better for atypical than typical actions. Replicating Black and Bower's work but taking these controls into account would make a challenging workshop.

A good part of the reading that most of you do is likely to be of textbooks, and other nonfiction materials rather than the fiction stories considered so far. These texts may also have somewhat regular structures which may be encoded in terms of something like a script. One quite difficult alternative would be to try to work out some of the likely scripts or frameworks that people use for nonfiction materials and to investigate their role in text processing. Presumably for psychology journal articles the accepted format could allow readers to develop a sort of framework, but for textbooks the position is less clear.

Reder and Anderson (1980) investigated nonfiction texts but they looked at the relation of texts to their summaries rather than for an abstract underlying structure. In particular, they compared the ease with which texts and their summaries can be processed and remembered. In general they found that summaries were remembered better and utilised more easily than complete texts. Why do authors bother writing texts rather than just summaries? It would be interesting to see whether Reder and Anderson's results can be replicated. You could also consider conditions in which subjects studied both texts and their summaries, or read the text and then generated their own summary. Reder and Anderson only tested memory for the main points which were included in the summaries. You might also check whether subjects who read the complete text gained additional, less central, information from it. You should consider how this relates to Black and Bower's finding that memory for superordinate actions or statements is superior to that for subordinate ones, and that memory for a superordinate action is improved by adding to the story additional actions subordinate to it.

Rather than looking at printed text, Keenan, MacWhinney, and Mayhew (1977) investigated pragmatic effects in memory for sentences from a naturally occurring group conversation. They compared memory for sentences with 'low interactional' content which made more or less factual statements about the world outside the conversation, with memory for those of 'high interactional' content which involved 'information about the speaker's intentions, his beliefs, and his relations with the listener' (p. 550). They tested memory after an interval of a day or two and found that both verbatim and gist memory were better for sentences with high interactional rather than low interactional content. As Keenan *et al.* pointed out, these findings are at variance with much laboratory-based research which reports quite poor verbatim memory after only a few seconds. This study is fascinating in looking at memory for naturally occurring conversation by the participants in that conversation. (How often have *you* argued over who said what in a previous conversation?) You might try to replicate this study, perhaps tape recording a discussion over coffee or in a seminar class in order to obtain the memory materials. Like Keenan *et al.* you would need at least one control group to ensure that your high and low interactional sentences are equally memorable out of context. You may be able to decide experimentally among the various theories Keenan *et al.* offered to explain their findings.

References

Black, J. B., and Bower, G. H. Episodes as chunks in narrative memory. *Journal of Verbal Learning and Verbal Behavior*, 1979, **18**, 309–18.

Graesser, A. C., Woll, S. B., Kowalski, D. J., and Smith, D. A. Memory for typical and atypical actions in scripted activities. *Journal of Experimental Psychology: Human Learning and Memory*, 1980, **6**, 503-15.

References for Alternatives

Keenan, J. M., MacWhinney, B., and Mayhew, D. Pragmatics in memory: A study of natural conversation. *Journal of Verbal Learning and Verbal Behavior*, 1977, **16**, 549-60.
Reder, L. M., and Anderson, J. R. A comparison of texts and their summaries: Memorial consequences. *Journal of Verbal Learning and Verbal Behavior*, 1980, **19**, 121-34.

VI
Thinking

Introduction

Thinking is an umbrella term used both in everyday and psychological contexts to cover a diversity of phenomena. In everyday terms, thinking applies to virtually any form of mental activity from daydreams to decision-making. In a psychological sense, too, the term has a wide scope. It refers to the processes involved in reasoning, problem-solving and creativity, as well as to forms of symbolic mental representation (e.g. images and knowledge).

Because of the complexity of the area, researchers have tended to concentrate on one aspect of thinking rather than cover the whole range of phenomena. As Greene (1975) remarks, 'what it usually comes down to is that, after a ritual bow to the richness of our mental life, discussion centres on just one type of thinking, namely problem solving' (p. 15). Of course, attention has also been given to other topics, notably reasoning and creativity, although some writers would argue that even these two topics can be viewed as specific examples of problem-solving behaviour.

When problem-solving is selected as the focus of attention, the task of studying what happens when we 'think' becomes easier. Some of the experimental paradigms used to study memory, for example, can be extended to the study of problem-solving. In some memory experiments, the experimenter decides what is to be remembered and tests how much is actually remembered. The composition of the memory lists, instructions and procedures can be altered to test hypotheses about the type of processes involved in remembering. Similarly, in experiments on problem-solving, the experimenter can define the problem and examine how many subjects solve it correctly. We can test the effect that different instructions and procedures have on subjects' ability to solve the same problem, or we can compare performance on different sorts of problems.

Problems can vary in the amount of thinking required to reach a solution. For example, a distinction is often made between problems of a mathematical type, where the subject knows a formula and needs only to substitute information in the formula to reach a solution, and problems like crosswords where there are often several alternative answers and the subject has to evaluate which fits. With both these types of problem, particularly the second, we can examine the sequence of decisions made by the subject (i.e. their protocol), and from this we can infer the subject's problem-solving strategy. Researchers interested in the computer simulation of thought processes are particularly concerned with protocol examination. They devise computer programs to generate possible solution strategies to problems. The protocols of human subjects are then compared to those produced by the computer. To set up the computer program in the first place requires, of course, a theory of the sorts of cognitive processes involved in the solution of the problem. One such program is the General Problem Solver. A discussion of this, as well as of protocol analysis techniques and computer simulation in general can be found in Newell and Simon (1972) and Simon (1979).

The study of thinking is distinguished in the cognitive processes area by an interest in the behaviour of individual subjects as well as of groups of subjects. Finding, for example, that a particular subject can solve one form of problem but not another has important implications for the generality of thought processes. Further, by examining the protocols of several different subjects solving the same problem, it soon becomes apparent that the same answer to a problem can be reached in many different ways. This observation applies not only to closed problems which have a clearly defined right answer, but also to open-ended problems with no one right answer. In open-ended problem situations, the subjects must define the extent of the problem for themselves! It is this sort of problem situation that is generally employed to study creative thought. Individual differences in problem-solving strategies for both open and closed problems have also attracted some interest from researchers investigating the nature of intelligence and intelligent behaviour (Resnick, 1976).

The workshops in this section cover problem-solving, reasoning, decision-making and creativity. The studies were chosen to illustrate some of the experimental approaches in the thinking area. Workshops T1 and T2 use designs similar to those employed in the study of memory. Workshops T3, T4 and T5 demonstrate the protocol analysis approach, and T6 and T7 examine thinking in open-ended contexts.

Workshops T1 and T2 examine the sorts of errors that subjects make on reasoning tasks. Analysis of the errors related to specific task variables, such as instructions and different problem types, provides insight into the sort of processes involved in reasoning. For example, in Workshop T1 subjects' ability to solve three-term series reasoning problems is related to their use of spatial imagery. In Workshop T2 errors in logical reasoning are shown to vary with the content of the argument. Subjects' judgments of validity may well be less accurate for those arguments about which they feel strongly.

Workshops T3, T4 and T5 all require the subject to make several overt choices while solving a problem. In Workshop T3 the popular Mastermind game is used to illustrate the strategies or sequence of moves used by subjects in a concept attainment situation. The concept is a particular set of coloured pegs chosen by one player, the experimenter. This study is linked to the concept attainment strategies reported by Bruner, Goodnow and Austin (1956).

Workshops T4 and T5 illustrate the technique of protocol analysis mentioned above. Workshop T4 asks whether human subjects use the same strategies as those generated by a computer to solve the Tower of Hanoi problem. Workshop T5 begins with a computer strategy, but focusses on the question of what is learned when we solve a problem. An Alternative for T4 uses protocol analysis to determine the strategies we use to solve everyday problems, for example, deciding a menu for a special dinner party. In conjunction with these three workshops, you might consider the recent debate on the validity of verbal reports and protocol analysis as data (Ericsson and Simon, 1980; Nisbett and Wilson, 1977).

How does creative thinking differ from the sort of thought processes examined in the other workshops? Workshop T6 examines whether or not it is possible to stimulate creative thinking either by providing a humorous atmosphere or by giving specific instructions that urge subjects to think of unconventional responses. Workshop T7 links problem-solving and thinking to everyday matters, by examining decision-making in a jury setting, selection procedures for job applicants and intuitive predictions about the frequency of particular events. Decision-making in social contexts is subject to several common biases which are of interest to both social and cognitive psychologists. You could consult Carroll and Payne (1976), Slovic, Fischhoff and Lichtenstein (1977) or Tversky and Kahneman (1974) for an introduction to this research.

Both Greene (1975) and Glass, Holyoak and Santa (1979) contain useful brief introductions to the main questions raised and methods employed in the study of thinking. Greene provides background material for the language workshops as well as the thinking workshops and in so doing supplies a theoretical link between the two areas. Glass *et al.* integrate their treatment of problem-solving, creativity and decision strategies with cognition in general, providing a text that is a useful reference for all the workshops in this book. There are many other texts and collections of readings that you could read subsequently to Greene and Glass *et al.*, for example, Bolton (1972), Johnson (1972), Johnson-Laird and Wason (1977), and Wason and Johnson-Laird (1968). If you are concerned about the application of problem-solving research to education, you might be interested in the book edited by Tuma and Reif (1980).

The study of thinking is complex and elusive. The workshops in this section illustrate some of the ways of investigating this sort of behaviour experimentally.

References

Bolton, N. *The Psychology of Thinking*. London: Methuen, 1972.

144   *Thinking*

Bruner, J. S., Goodnow, J. J., and Austin, G. A. *A Study of Thinking*. New York: Wiley, 1956.

Carroll, J. S., and Payne, J. W. (eds). *Cognition and Social Behavior*. Hillsdale, New Jersey: Lawrence Erlbaum Associates, 1976.

Ericsson, K. A., and Simon, H. A. Verbal reports as data. *Psychological Review*, 1980, **87**, 215–51.

Glass, A. L., Holyoak, K. J., and Santa, J. L. *Cognition*, Reading, Mass.: Addison-Wesley, 1979.

Greene, J. *Thinking and Language*. London: Methuen, 1975.

Johnson, D. M. *A Systematic Introduction to the Psychology of Thinking*. New York: Harper & Row, 1972.

Johnson-Laird, P. N., and Wason, P. C. (eds). *Thinking: Readings in Cognitive Science*. Cambridge: Cambridge University Press, 1977.

Newell, A., and Simon, H. A. *Human Problem Solving*. Englewood Cliffs, New Jersey: Prentice-Hall, 1972.

Nisbett, R. E., and Wilson, T. D. Telling more than we can know: Verbal reports on mental processes. *Psychological Review*, 1977, **84**, 231–59.

Resnick, L. B. (ed.). *The Nature of Intelligence*. Hillsdale, New Jersey: Lawrence Erlbaum Associates, 1976.

Simon, H. A. Information processing models of cognition. *Annual Review of Psychology*, 1979, **30**, 363–96.

Slovic, P., Fischhoff, B., and Lichtenstein, S. Behavioral decision theory. *Annual Review of Psychology*, 1977, **28**, 1–39.

Tuma, D. T., and Reif, F. (eds). *Problem-solving and Education: Issues in Teaching and Research*. Hillsdale, New Jersey: Lawrence Erlbaum Associates, 1980.

Tversky, A., and Kahneman, D. Judgment under uncertainty: Heuristics and biases. *Science*, 1974, **185**, 1124–31.

Wason, P. C. and Johnson-Laird, P. N. (eds). *Thinking and Reasoning*. Harmondsworth: Penguin, 1968.

T1 Three-term series problems

Do we think in images?

> IXL is cheaper than SPC
> IXL is dearer than PMU
> Which brand is the dearest?

You can almost feel the 'cogs' turning when this question is asked. Trying to reach a solution becomes difficult as names become confused and you find yourself asking 'What brand was cheaper than SPC?' 'What was the name of the other brand?' This is especially so if there are more than three items to compare.

Of course, the problem is much easier if you have the cans or bottles in front of you on the supermarket shelf. There you would probably collect the items together, order them from dearest to cheapest, then make a decision. This spatial manipulation strategy fits a model, proposed by Huttenlocher and Higgins (1971) to explain how we solve these sorts of problems. They suggested that we combine the information from the two sentences or premises by imagining a spatial array and ordering names or items in that array.

Several experiments have shown that these problems are easier if the information in the premises can be ordered from the top of an array, downwards (e.g. A is taller than B: B is taller than C), or from the end-points to the centre (e.g. A is taller than B: C is shorter than B). Huttenlocher and Higgins suggested that these findings reflect our spatial ordering preferences.

Shaver, Pierson and Lang (1975) outlined several experimental procedures that allow us to test Huttenlocher and Higgins's theory that we use spatial imagery to order the items in this sort of problem. For instance, if subjects are using spatial imagery it should be possible to interfere with their imaging by presenting the problems visually rather than aurally. Further, subjects who are rated good imagers should perform better than subjects who are poor imagers. Shaver *et al.* found support for both of these proposals and added that the use and effectiveness of an imagery strategy should also vary with the sort of instructions given to subjects and the particular relations involved in the problems. Both Huttenlocher and Higgins and Shaver *et al.* pointed out that some comparative adjectives (e.g. taller-shorter, better-worse) seem to be more suited to spatial ordering than others (e.g. lighter-darker).

This workshop specifically examines Shaver *et al.*'s suggestion (p. 317) that although imagery may not be necessary to solve three-term series problems, it is nevertheless a very useful strategy. In a replication of their second experiment, some subjects in this workshop will be given special instructions to use imagery to solve a set of problems, while others will be given no specific hints. We might expect the performance of those subjects using an imagery strategy to vary, depending on the particular comparative adjective used and on the ordering of information in the premises. Studying how we solve these three-term series problems should throw some light on everyday reasoning exercises, for example, comparative shopping in the supermarket, or decisions about the relative chances of horses in a race.

General procedure

Following Shaver *et al.*'s design, you will need a set of 32 problems – 16 using the comparative adjectives better-worse and 16 using lighter-darker. Shaver *et al.* also varied the order of information in the premises. For example:

1   Top, downwards: A is better than B: B is better than C. Is A better than C?
2   Bottom, upwards: C is worse than B: B is worse than A. Is C worse than A?
3   End-points to centre: A is better than B: C is worse than B. Is C better than A?
4   Centre, outwards: B is worse than A: B is better than C. Is C better than A?

If you use these four types of problems (i.e. premise combination and question), you will be able to compare your data on the percentage of correct responses, with previous findings listed in Shaver *et al.* (p. 362). Four examples of each type of problem are needed for each adjective (i.e. a total of 16 problems for each comparative adjective).

You might decide to use another comparative adjective as well. Huttenlocher and Higgins offered some suggestions for alternatives. It is best, though, to limit the number of problems to between 30 and 40, since the task is fairly demanding of subjects. You will need two or three extra problems for practice trials.

The problems, presented in random order, can either be recorded on tape or read aloud by the experimenter. Allow ten seconds between each problem for subjects to answer 'Yes/No' to the questions.

Randomly assign your subjects to two groups, corresponding to the instructions given regarding the solution of the problems. You can get ideas for the imagery instructions from both Huttenlocher and Higgins, and Shaver *et al.* The control subjects are simply encouraged to answer as accurately as possible. Depending on your available space and time, you could either print instructions on separate response sheets and distribute these to the group without alerting subjects to variation in treatment, or run the two conditions separately.

You might like to ask subjects about their strategies at the end of the experiment, following Shaver *et al.* (pp. 364 and 372). This provides one way of checking on whether the control subjects were also using an imagery strategy.

The design is a 2 (instructions) × 2 (adjectives) × 4 (problem type) factorial with repeated measures on the last two factors. To compare your results with those reported by Shaver *et al.* (pp. 362 and 372) you will need to calculate the average number of errors for each instruction group and the percentage of correct responses in each cell. To make scoring easier, prepare a master response sheet with the correct answers, and code for the different cells (e.g. whether this answer contributes to adjective *A*, problem type 2, etc.).

In the discussion you should consider the success of the imagery instructions. Did subjects find it easy to use the strategy? Were the control subjects also using that strategy? Were there any reports of different strategies? You could also discuss the importance of individual variation in explaining performance on this task (cf. Shaver *et al.*, p. 373). Some writers, including Shaver *et al.*, suggest that subjects might change their strategies as they become more experienced with the task. How would you test to determine whether there were changes? In addition, our experience suggests that it would be interesting to look closely for any practice effects.

Alternatives

You might try the interference procedure used in the first experiment of Shaver *et al.* The problems were presented visually to some subjects and aurally to others, and Shaver *et al.* reported significant main effects and some interaction effects. More errors occurred with visual presentation, and especially with those problems involving a spatial relation (e.g. tall-short), giving support to the theory that subjects were using imagery to solve the problems. For the visual condition, Shaver *et al.* filmed the problems, but you could perhaps use a computer-controlled display screen, slides, an overhead projector or a memory drum instead.

References

Huttenlocher, J., and Higgins, E. T. Adjectives, comparatives and syllogisms. *Psychological Review*, 1971, **78**, 487–504.
Shaver, P., Pierson, L., and Lang, S. Converging evidence for the functional significance of imagery in problem-solving. *Cognition*, 1975, **3**, 359–75.

T2 Deductive reasoning
How does emotion affect our logic?

Consider the following statement:

Women don't think logically because they are swayed by emotion and
as we all know, logical thinkers do not allow themselves to be influenced
by emotion.

Although women may want to deny this popular stereotype, the argument is actually valid. This is not, of course, to say that the premises and
hence the conclusion are true. Male chauvinists take heed! Often in daily
life we tend to rely on our attitude toward the content when evaluating an
argument rather than the validity of the inferences involved. Advertisers
can use this characteristic to advantage, creating associations like 'All these
show-winning dogs eat brand X dogfood', and calculating that consumers
will add 'My dog will be a show-winner too because I feed him brand X'.
The argument is of course invalid, but how many cans of brand X are sold
because owners would like to think that their dog could be a show-winner?
This distinction between the validity of an argument and an individual's
belief in the truth or falsity of a conclusion is important to note. The form
of a valid argument is such that whenever its premises are true, its conclusions *must* be true. For an invalid argument there is no such link between
the truth or falsity of its premises and the truth or falsity of its conclusions.
So, if a valid argument has a false conclusion (e.g. women never think logically) then it *must* have a false premise (i.e. logical thinkers are never
swayed by emotion).
To illustrate this distinction and the reasoning errors that arise. Lefford
(1946) asked college students to judge both the validity of a set of syllogisms
and the truth or falsity of the conclusions of those syllogisms. The syllogisms differed in subject matter. Some were based on socially or politically
controversial topics likely to excite an emotional judgment, while others
contained neutral material (e.g. the use of barometers to gauge weather
changes). Lefford found that subjects made fewer reasoning errors on the
neutrally toned syllogisms and that the subjects' judgment that a conclusion
was true tended to bias their judgment of validity. So, for instance, if a

subject agreed with the conclusion, he or she was more likely to judge the argument as valid: if a subject disagreed with the conclusion, he or she tended to judge the argument as invalid. This was true for both emotional and neutral syllogisms.

This workshop is based on Lefford's study. We are interested in the effect of two factors on syllogistic reasoning – (1) the subject's agreement with the conclusion, and (2) the content of the argument: i.e. emotional versus neutral topics.

General procedure

Generating a set of syllogisms is the most difficult part of this study. There should be enough information presented below and in the references to help those of you who have not done a course in logic, but you will need to devote a fair amount of time to this task.

For a description of the various forms of syllogisms you can refer to any introductory logic text book with a section on either syllogistic reasoning or symbolic logic. You might also refer to a summary included in Chapman and Chapman (1959) which contains the main points you will need for this workshop.

For simplicity's sake, four valid syllogistic forms and four invalid syllogistic forms are set out below. You can use these to generate your set of syllogisms, or if this is too difficult, select appropriate examples from Lefford. Of course, if you have some expertise in this area, you could use other forms, based either on syllogistic or symbolic argument forms.

Four Valid Forms

1
No M is P
All S is M
Therefore no S is P

2
No P is M
Some S is M
Therefore some S is not P

3
All M are P
All M are S
Therefore some S are P

4
All P are M   (Premise 1)
No M is S   (Premise 2)
Therefore no S is P   (Conclusion)

Four Invalid Forms

5
All M is P
Some S is M
Therefore some S is not P

6
All P is M
All S is M
Therefore all S is P

7
Some M is not P
All M are S
Therefore no S is P

8
All P is M
Some M is S
Therefore no S is P

To generate your set of syllogisms, replace each of the three letters, *S, P* and *M* with a term which can be a category, a name or a property. Take care to be consistent in substitution within each argument. You will need one emotionally toned version and one neutral version for each of these eight forms. Here are some emotional and neutral examples of the valid and invalid forms listed above.

Valid form (1): Emotional

No politician is really honest
Malcolm Fraser is a politician
Therefore Malcolm Fraser is not really honest

(Note that 'all' in the second premise can be replaced by a proper name or a set of names, i.e. implying 'all Malcolm Frasers'.)

For the emotionally toned syllogisms, it might be better to state the conclusion first, especially if your subjects are not likely to believe it. So:

Malcolm Fraser is not really honest because he is a politician, and, after all, no politicians are really honest.

Valid form (3): Neutral

All whales are mammals and they all swim, therefore some creatures that can swim are mammals.

Invalid form (6): Emotional

All socialists favour bank nationalisation
Labor Party supporters favour bank nationalisation
Therefore Labor Party supporters are socialists.

Or stated differently:

Labor Party supporters are really socialists because they favour bank nationalisation and all socialists favour bank nationalisation.

Contrast this syllogism to an analogous neutral version:

Invalid form (6): Neutral

All whales are mammals
All kangaroos are mammals
Therefore all kangaroos are whales.

When generating your syllogisms, you will also need to consider the content of the conclusions. For example, the conclusion — all kangaroos are whales — is obviously false, and as Lefford and others suggest, this is likely to bias the subject's judgment of the validity of the argument. To test this proposal you will need to vary the apparent truth/falsity of the conclusion to your syllogisms. The easiest way to do this is to generate your emotional syllogisms so that the four valid forms have apparently false conclusions and the four invalid forms have apparently true conclusions. This will ensure that subjects making validity judgments on the basis of the apparent truth of the conclusions will always produce errors for these emotional syllogisms. You could use the neutral syllogisms as a control (i.e. have all the conclusions true). This simplification partially confounds the truth of conclusions variable with emotionality. A more complicated design which avoids this problem is mentioned in the alternatives section. It is, of course, easier to determine which conclusions are likely to be seen as true or false for the neutral syllogisms than for the emotional syllogisms. You could, perhaps, ask some friends to judge the statements prior to the study and accept a consensus.

For this study, you can use a repeated measures design, presenting each subject with 16 syllogisms — 8 emotionally toned and 8 neutral, matched for valid and invalid forms. If you decide to use argument forms other than those listed above, take care to match the syllogistic forms across the emotional and neutral versions.

The syllogisms could be printed one per page, and stapled to form a booklet. This would enable you to present the syllogisms in a different random order for each subject. Use Lefford's instructions as a guide to devising your own. He asked subjects first to judge the validity of the arguments (that is, whether or not 'the conclusions can justifiably be drawn from the premises'). After making these judgments, subjects were asked to go back over the conclusions and indicate whether, in their opinion, the conclusions were True or False.

Simply calculate the average number of incorrect validity judgments for the emotional syllogisms and the average number of incorrect validity judgments for the neutral arguments. Do subjects make more errors when judging emotional arguments? In addition, you could enter each syllogism into a 2 × 2 contingency table (conclusions judged true or false × arguments judged valid or invalid) and then calculate a chi-square to see whether subjects do tend to judge arguments as valid or invalid depending on whether they see the conclusion as true or false.

If you have both males and females in your sample, you could check the results for sex differences. Is there any support for the syllogism that opened this workshop? In discussion, you might ask why most people find these syllogisms, especially the emotionally toned versions, so difficult.

Henle (1962) argues that these reasoning errors do not necessarily indicate that subjects are unable to think logically. She suggests that when syllogisms are presented on everyday or controversial topics, subjects do not see the problem as one requiring the application of logical rules. How might you investigate this suggestion?

Alternatives

To separate the three variables — apparent truth or falsity of conclusion, validity or invalidity of argument and emotional or neutral content — you would need a 2 × 2 × 2 design. Again you can use a repeated measures procedure, obtaining a score for each subject in each cell. A multiple regression analysis would allow you to see whether emotionality or truth/falsity was the most important variable or whether both variables contribute equally to the judgments of the arguments.

You might be interested in examining the 'atmosphere effect' (Chapman and Chapman, 1959). This effect refers to the finding that subjects tend to use the 'atmosphere' created by the words 'all', 'some' and 'no' in the premises as a guide to judging the conclusions. Chapman and Chapman find that, for syllogisms like Valid form 1 above, subjects are biassed towards selecting a negative conclusion in a multiple-choice task. You could consider Johnson-Laird and Steedman's (1978) criticisms of this 'atmosphere' theory.

Another way to investigate reasoning ability is simply to present subjects with pairs of premises and ask them to generate logical conclusions. Johnson-Laird and Steedman (1978) argue that this is a better way to investigate reasoning, since subjects who are asked to judge the validity of an argument could simply decide by guessing rather than by making inferences. Using this method, Johnson-Laird and Steedman find both variation in the difficulty of problems and a bias toward particular forms of conclusions being linked to particular patterns of premises, i.e. a figural effect. For example, for the Valid form 1 there is a bias towards having the terms in the conclusion ordered S-P, while for the Valid form 4, the bias is P-S. This figural effect can override the actual validity of the argument.

It would be interesting to see if this pattern of results still arose when the truth and content of the premises were manipulated. The results of such a study would have important implications for the theory of syllogistic reasoning outlined by Johnson-Laird and Steedman. You might ask your subjects how they did the task. Do their explanations fit Johnson-Laird and Steedman's theory?

References

Chapman, L. J., and Chapman, J. P. Atmosphere effect re-examined. *Journal of Experimental Psychology*, 1959, **58**, 220–6.

Henle, E. On the relation between logic and thinking. *Psychological Review*, 1962, **69**, 366–78.

Lefford, A. The influence of emotional subject matter on logical reasoning. *Journal of General Psychology*, 1946, **34**, 127–51.

Reference for Alternatives

Johnson-Laird, P. N., and Steedman, M. The psychology of syllogisms. *Cognitive Psychology*, 1978, **10**, 64–99.

T3 Concept-attainment strategies

Are you a mastermind?

When writing an essay on a particular topic, what strategy do you adopt? Do you scan many articles for ideas or select one paper and focus on its contents? Or do you combine these strategies, perhaps beginning with a scanning approach and ending with a focus approach?

Variations of these two information-selecting strategies were employed by subjects in Bruner, Goodnow and Austin's (1956) concept-attainment studies. These studies used a familiar parlour-game setting in which one player (the subject) must work out a concept chosen by another player (the experimenter). In this case, the subject was first shown one card which illustrated an example of the experimenter's concept, and was then asked to select other cards from a large array to determine the exact nature of the concept. The subject was told after each choice whether or not the card was an example of the concept. Each card in the array varied systematically on some attributes (for example, number, shape and colour of the figures drawn on the card).

Bruner, Goodnow and Austin used the term *strategy* to refer to the pattern of decisions or card selections made by the subjects. The task described above provided a record of card selections, and so allowed an easy analysis of strategies. Bruner, Goodnow and Austin report that some subjects focussed on the first or previously selected card, and chose other instances so that they varied just on one attribute (conservative focussing) or on a few attributes (focus gambling). Other subjects formed hypotheses about the concept, choosing cards either to test one hypothesis (successive scanning) or to test several possibilities (simultaneous scanning).

Because these strategies involve varying amounts of cognitive strain (e.g. memory load), information feedback and probabilities of success/failure, Bruner, Goodnow and Austin suggested that whether a focus or a scan strategy is adopted is determined largely by the task demands. For example, if the number of choices is limited to say four, then you would expect, as Bruner, Goodnow and Austin found, that subjects take a riskier approach, varying several attributes at once. Where there are no time pressures, and no limit to the number of choices, subjects are more likely to adopt the conservative focussing strategy, where some information is guaranteed with each choice. Further, it is reported that subjects who select a series of positive instances are more likely to change to a riskier strategy.

Johnson (1978) presented a detailed critique of the manner in which Bruner, Goodnow and Austin determined and described their subjects' strategies. He argued that if focussing and scanning are valid examples of general problem-solving strategies, then the concepts should be useful in describing and predicting subjects' behaviour on other tasks.

As a test of the generality of the selection strategies described by Bruner, Goodnow and Austin, it would be interesting to see whether or not subjects use similar sorts of strategies in a game marketed under the name 'Mastermind'. In this game one player (the subject) must work out the position and colours of five pegs chosen by another player (the experimenter). For each move, the subject chooses a set of five pegs and is then given information about the number of correct colours he or she has selected and whether these correct colours are in the correct position. A record is kept on a board of the subjects' sequence of moves and the feedback for each move.

It would also be interesting to see if the type of strategy adopted by subjects playing Mastermind is affected by particular task demands as Bruner, Goodnow and Austin suggested. For example, can subjects in the Mastermind game follow a focus strategy if specifically instructed to do so? When restricted to only four moves, do subjects adopt a riskier strategy? This workshop is designed to investigate these questions.

General procedure

It is relatively easy to construct your own version of the game, if you do not have access to the commercial variety. For example, you can design a response sheet with rows of circles. Subjects, then, can either use coloured pencils to fill in the circles or simply write the name of the colour in each circle. The game could also be played with numbers or any other set of items. Johnson's Hits and Misses game, for instance, is similar to Mastermind and uses a sequence of four letters selected from the first eight of the alphabet. You will need to decide the number of items in your sequence (four or five are probably sufficiently difficult) and the size of the set from which they are selected (e.g. six to eight). The experimenter can use ticks and crosses, or some other symbols, to provide the feedback information: for example, in Mastermind a tick indicates that both colour and position are correct; a cross indicates that only the colour is correct.

Feedback is given for each item correct, but in a random order (i.e. the experimenter does not draw his ticks and crosses in order, left to right, to correspond with the subject's line of items). In this game, the experimenter needs to take special care that accurate feedback information is given.

With only five positions and a range of eight possible colours, the game is fairly difficult (there are 32,768 permutations), so for our purposes it is probably best to limit the choice of a row to five different colours (i.e. no repeated colours or empty positions). Further, instruct all subjects to begin by selecting five different colours (meaning that they will have at least two bits of positive feedback from their first move). Obviously, you will need to tell subjects about the sort of feedback information they will be given.

As well as these general instructions, subjects can be given some special instructions to alter the task demands. Your decision on whether or not to include these manipulations will depend on the specific hypotheses you want to test in this study and the availability of time, subjects and experimenters. One group, for example, might simply be told to use any strategy they like, while another group can be restricted to a small number of moves (e.g. four). A third group might be specifically instructed to use a focussing strategy. An example of this sort of strategy follows. You may include this in your instructions, or devise one of your own, following the description given by Bruner, Goodnow and Austin (ch. 4) or by Johnson.

On each move you should introduce only one *new* colour and change the position of *one* old colour from the previous move. All other colours and positions are held constant.

| For example: | (1) | X | X | Red | X | Blue |
| | (2) | X | X | Blue | X | White |

To follow this strategy exactly, you must put the new colour (white) in the same position as the old colour that is changing position (blue). Blue then changes to the position of the discarded colour (red).

In response to your move, the experimenter can now add or withdraw crosses or ticks or leave the feedback unchanged. From this feedback you can make inferences about the two changed items:
(a) If the experimenter *adds a cross/tick*, then the new colour/position must be correct and the old one incorrect.
(b) If the experimenter leaves the number of *crosses unchanged*, then you know that either the new and old colours are both correct *or* both incorrect.
(c) If the experimenter leaves the number of *ticks unchanged*, then either the new and old colours and positions are both correct *or* both incorrect.
(d) If the experimenter *withdraws a cross/tick*, then the new colour/ position is incorrect and the old one correct.

Following (d) the old colour can be returned to a position held previously without counting as a change. When you are close to the end and you *know* the correct sequence, you can change several things at once.

If you decide to use this strategy, allow the subject several practice trials before beginning the game. This strategy, if followed exactly, should lead to a solution in five to seven moves.

If your testing time is limited to the laboratory session, you could arrange for players to work in pairs, taking turns to act as subject and experimenter. Otherwise you could test each subject individually. In both cases, you might also have each subject solve several problems.

Since our interest lies in the strategies adopted by subjects, ideally we should both analyse the pattern of moves made by each subject to classify them as a scanner or a focusser, and try to distinguish these strategies on some critical performance variables. The first approach requires a fairly complicated analysis so you should tackle this only if you have the time, or perhaps you could analyse just one or two subjects' protocols in this way. Otherwise, it is probably best to concentrate on the second approach, following the suggestions of Johnson, and Bruner, Goodnow and Austin. You can calculate, for instance, the number of moves required for solution and the number of changes made on the first move (for the focussing strategy outlined, this would equal two). It might also be interesting to keep a record of the time taken by each subject to make each move, and to compare the average time for the different instruction groups. The distribution of these measures could be graphed (see Johnson p. 247).

Do the special instructions or the strategies adopted by your subjects lead to differences between the groups on the various measures? Do the strategies impose different levels of cognitive strain, and is this reflected in the performance measures taken or in subjects' own impressions? During discussion, you might ask those subjects who were not instructed to use a specific strategy whether or not they were working to a particular plan. Do some subjects seem to change strategies in the course of the game? You might also discuss the problems that you faced in attempting to classify subjects as scanners or focussers in the light of Johnson's arguments about the validity of these strategy descriptions. Does experience in playing this game change performance?

Alternatives

You could consider making a detailed analysis of each subject's protocol, checking to see for instance:

1 if there was any evidence of a change in strategy,
2 whether or not strategy changes are related to the sort of feedback received (e.g. increased positive v. negative).
3 if subjects take advantage of negative information.

As well as focussers and scanners, Johnson identified tacticians and blunderers. Do these extra strategy descriptions fit with your data?

Johnson's procedure differed from that of Bruner, Goodnow and Austin on several important features. His subjects played against a computer which varied the sequence being sought, depending on the decisions made by the subject. Subjects could either select a sequence or announce a hypothesis. They were given a list of all possible hypotheses and could make notes of ideas as they worked through the problem. There were no time restrictions or limit to the number of moves.

If you have a computer available you might replicate his three games: Zaps and Duds, Odd Ball, and Hits and Misses. Alternatively, you could have subjects play these games with a human (here the correct sequence would remain unchanged throughout the problem), or you could allow subjects in the Mastermind game to either make a move or announce a hypothesis. This might better enable you to distinguish scanners from focussers. Johnson, for instance, suggested that scanners are more likely to announce hypotheses. You could also encourage subjects to write down the reasons for their decisions. This would give you more information on which to judge the strategy they were using.

Bruner, Goodnow and Austin (ch. 4) used both abstract concepts (i.e. pictures of squares, circles, etc.) and thematic concepts (pictures of adults and children). They report that different strategies prevailed with the thematic cards. You could replicate this finding, using Word Mastermind, for instance. In this version of the game, the subject's task is to determine a five- or six-letter word chosen by the experimenter. Feedback is given on the number of correct letters, and the number of correct letters in their right position. Are subjects more likely to adopt a scanning strategy that tests successive or simultaneous hypotheses, when the material is more familiar? What implication would this result have for Johnson's proposal that the identification of an individual as a focusser or a scanner on one task should reflect that individual's normal problem-solving style on similar tasks?

References

Bruner, J. S., Goodnow, J. J., and Austin, G. A. *A Study of Thinking*. New York: Wiley, 1956 (ch. 4).

Johnson, E. S. Validation of concept-learning strategies. *Journal of Experimental Psychology: General*, 1978, **107**, 237–72.

T4 The Tower of Hanoi problem

Do humans solve problems as computers do?

> If we are to understand human problem-solving behavior, we must get a
> solid grip on the strategies that underlie that behavior, and we must
> avoid blending together in a statistical stew quite diverse problem-solving
> behaviors whose real significance is lost in the averaging process. (Simon,
> 1975, p. 288)

An experiment in cognitive psychology generally involves setting up several
treatment groups, obtaining one or more scores from individual subjects,
then averaging across subjects within each group. In a study of problem-
solving, for example, we might compare the groups on the number of
correct solutions, or time taken to reach a solution. Many people would
argue, along with Simon (1975), that this procedure misses the important
data of problem-solving, namely individual differences. Subjects might reach
the same solution by different routes. Simon uses computer-generated
solutions of the Tower of Hanoi problem to illustrate this possibility.

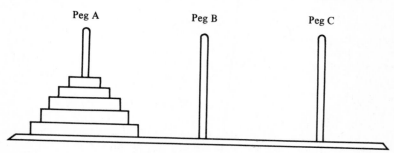

Figure 1: Model of the Tower of Hanoi problem

In the Tower of Hanoi problem (see Fig. 1) the task is to move a pyra-
mid of N discs from peg A to peg C, with the constraints (a) that only one
disc can be moved at a time, and (b) that a disc cannot be placed on top of
a disc that is smaller than itself. The minimum number of moves is $2^N - 1$,
where N is the number of discs.

In generating his strategies, Simon makes several assumptions about the steps taken by human subjects in their search for a solution. For instance, he assumes that no attempt is made to solve the problem until the instructions are fully understood (Simon and Hayes, 1976), and that since different strategies place different demands on memory processes, the choice of a particular solution strategy is determined by the task environment. We might expect different strategies, for example, when subjects are required to solve the problem in their heads rather than on paper or with the aid of a model. Subjects who can move discs on a model have to remember only the sequence of moves they have made. Those people who are required to do the problem in their heads, need to remember both the sequence of moves and the current position of discs on pegs. Given these memory constraints, it would follow from Simon's assumption that subjects working in their heads adopt a strategy that is different from those subjects who work with a model. Further, we might predict that those subjects who solve the problem on paper are more likely to detect Simon's (1975) move-pattern strategy, since only these subjects have a readily accessible record of the sequence of their moves. They can simply look at their written records to refresh their memory.

To test these assumptions we need to compare the computer-generated strategies with the actual performance of human subjects, and that means devising a way of gaining a record or protocol of each subject's solution steps. One way to do this is to ask subjects to either think aloud or think on paper (Simon and Hayes, 1976).

General procedure

This workshop will compare the protocols of subjects asked to solve the Tower of Hanoi problem in different task environments, with computer-generated strategies outlined by Simon (1975). Since this involves individual subject analysis, the presentation and write-up of the workshop is a little complicated. It is probably better to collect and analyse some protocols before the workshop session, and to use these to demonstrate particular strategies in your class discussion.

All subjects are initially given a description of the problem, noting especially the move constraints. You will need to decide the type of protocol collected either written or spoken and the number of task environments to be compared. These decisions will depend mainly on the time you have available for collecting and analysing data.

For a spoken protocol, you will need either to test each subject individually so that you can note down their comments, or have subjects record their moves on a tape recorder. Specifically instruct subjects to concentrate on thinking aloud. For this type of record, you could have some subjects moving discs on a model as they talk, others simply imagining the model, and perhaps some making notes on paper as they talk. A model of the problem is easily constructed with cardboard and pegs (or pencils) or with coins and circles. Four or five discs make the problem sufficiently difficult.

If you decide on a written protocol, instruct subjects to note all their thoughts on paper, and to indicate the temporal sequence of each thought by listing them down the page or by numbering each idea.

As an initial analysis, you could score, for each task environment, the proportion of subjects correctly solving the problem and the average number of moves used. It might be interesting to compare the average time taken by subjects to solve the problem as well. Having collected these data, you could then embark on the more complicated comparison of individual protocols with Simon's computer-generated strategies. The extent of this comparison will depend on the time available. You could, for example, just report global similarities/differences in the move sequences adopted by subjects in the various task environments, *or* present a specific analysis of the strategy adopted by each subject.

Are there any similarities between your subjects' protocols and Simon's computer-generated strategies? Did the various task environments lead to different strategies, and were those subjects working on paper more likely to detect the move-pattern strategy? You might base your discussion around the points raised by Greene (1975) on the computer simulation approach to problem-solving. You might also consider whether or not written or spoken protocols represent all the mental solution steps taken by human subjects in solving a problem. How else could we tap individual strategies?

Alternatives

It might be interesting to have some subjects produce a written and others a spoken protocol. Then you could compare the effect of different task environments in terms of (1) the demands placed on memory and (2) the amount of feedback available on the sequence of moves taken. For example, a heavy load is placed on subjects who imagine the model and voice their moves. The processing load is lightened when discs can be moved on the model, but subjects still have to remember the sequence of moves made. Those working on paper have a record of their moves, and those working on paper and with the model have two sources of information.

The Monsters and Globes problem (Simon and Hayes, 1976) is an interesting alternative to the Tower of Hanoi. This analogue could be used if your subjects indicate that they are familiar with the solution of the Tower of Hanoi. Simon and Hayes consider two versions of the Monster problem — one where the globes are transferred between monsters (a transfer problem, similar to the Tower of Hanoi) and the other where the globes remain constant while the monsters change in size (a change problem). They report that change problems are more difficult than transfer problems. You might set up a study to test this difference, following on from the ideas presented in their paper.

In solving complex problems like the Tower of Hanoi, most of us adopt some sort of 'means–ends' strategy, dividing the problem into several steps or sub-goals. If we have selected the appropriate sub-goals then we need only work through each step to reach the solution. This sort of strategy is common in everyday problem-solving. Byrne (1977) for example, presents a detailed analysis of the mental steps his subjects took in planning a series of dinner parties. Although some menus were recalled as a chunk (e.g. Christmas dinner), mostly subjects set up a series of sub-goals, considering each course and the relationship between courses, before making a final decision on a menu. You could either replicate Byrne's task or see if his analysis of decision strategies applied to similar everyday problems, for example buying Christmas presents for the family or planning which clothes to pack for a weekend trip. In replicating Byrne, you could see whether your subjects segmented the task in the way that Byrne's did. It is interesting to note the extra complications Byrne faces in analysing real-life problem-solving.

References

Greene, J. *Thinking and Language.* London: Methuen, 1975 (pp. 58–62).

Simon, H. A. The functional equivalence of problem-solving skills. *Cognitive Psychology*, 1975, 7, 268–88.

Simon, H. A., and Hayes, J. R. The understanding process: Problem isomorphs. *Cognitive Psychology*, 1976, 8, 165–90.

Reference for Alternatives

Byrne, R., Planning meals: Problem-solving on a real data-base. *Cognition*, 1977, 5, 287–332.

T5 The Missionaries and Cannibals problem

How do you cross bridges before you come to them?

It is often said that we learn from experience. Indeed, we often make allowances for this idea, providing a series of practice trials before an experiment proper. But just what sort of experience is useful and what do we learn?

What, for example, do we learn when we solve a problem like the Missionaries and Cannibals puzzle? The problem here is to transport three (or more) missionaries and three (or more) cannibals from one side of a river to the other in a boat that holds a maximum of two people. Since the boat must be rowed across the river, there must be at least one person in the boat on each journey. No missionaries may ever be left with a larger number of cannibals (either on the bank or in the boat) for the cannibals would overpower and eat the missionaries. An easy-to-follow flow diagram illustrating the sequence of legal moves for the problem and examples of illegal moves, can be found in Jeffries, Polson, Razran and Atwood (1977, p. 414). They outlined several theories about the strategies we use to solve such problems.

Reed, Ernst and Banerji (1974) asked whether or not the experience of having previously solved the Missionaries and Cannibals problem would have any effect on the number of moves taken and the time required either to solve the same problem again, or to solve an analogous problem. They report some positive transfer effects when subjects solved the same problem. However, when subjects solved an analogous problem there was little transfer, as measured by solution time and number of errors, unless subjects were specifically told of the relationship between the problems. These results still leave us with the question 'What is learned?'.

To begin to answer this question we might consider each move or step in the solution of the problem. In a problem like Missionaries and Cannibals there may be critical points where several alternative legal moves are possible. Here subjects have a choice between moves that take them further towards or away from the solution. Jeffries *et al.* found two such critical decision points (states 5 and 8) in their analysis of problems analogous to Missionaries and Cannibals. When moving from these states subjects were more likely to make an illegal move or an error. If subjects do learn something at these decision points, then on subsequent solutions of the same or similar problems, we might expect at these points both a decrease in the errors made and the time taken to decide on a move.

This workshop modifies the procedures used by Jeffries *et al*. and Reed *et al*. to allow for group testing in a single laboratory session. The general aim of this workshop lies in determining which performance indices change when subjects have previous experience in a particular task. These indices may suggest just what it is we learn when we learn to solve a problem.

General procedure

For this study, one group of subjects will solve the same problem twice: another will solve one problem followed by an analogous problem. You might decide to use any two of the six versions described in the articles (Missionaries and Cannibals, Jealous Husbands and Wives, Elves and Men-1 and -11, Hobbits and Orcs, or Silver and Gold) *or* you could make up an analogue of your own. When deciding on the particular problems to use, you might keep in mind (i) that Jeffries *et al*. found different patterns of errors in their four versions; and (ii) that Reed *et al*. found a transfer effect only for those subjects who solved Jealous Husbands and Wives first. These are fairly difficult problems so it is probably better to have only three of each sort of creature or object to be transported. You can then set a time limit of 30–45 minutes during which both problems should be solved.

Subjects could work in pairs with one solving the problems while the other keeps a record of the time taken to decide each step and checks on the legality of the moves. Alternatively, if you have two experimenters, each one could monitor two or three subjects at a time.

You will need to prepare instruction sheets outlining the problem(s) and design a response sheet giving a format for reporting solution steps. To make scoring easier, for example, you might have subjects use a flow chart format and notation similar to that printed in Jeffries *et al*. (p. 414). This would enable subjects to see a record of their previous moves. You will have to decide whether or not to inform subjects who solve the analogous problem of the relationship between the problems. Perhaps you could tell just half of them about the analogy, and ask the others at the end of the experiment if they recognised the relationship. Reed *et al*. also asked subjects at the end of their experiment to indicate which of four strategies (p. 444) they had used to solve the second problem.

Some aspects of this study are quite easy to score; others, more complicated. You will need to decide which measures suit your purposes and time limitations. For example, you could simply compare group data for each problem: calculating the average number of moves, the average time required to solve the problem, and the average number of illegal, backward and error moves. For a more detailed analysis you might follow Jeffries *et al*. and separately graph the mean number of error, illegal and backward moves and the time taken to respond for each state in the solution sequence.

You will need to prepare these graphs for both problems so that a comparison can be made. Did subjects find some steps in the solution of the problem more difficult? Did they cope better with the second problem especially at these difficult decision points (i.e. fewer errors and less time taken?

Were there any other indications of transfer between the two attempts at solving the problems? Did those subjects who were not informed recognise the relationship between the analogous problems? The subjects in both the Jeffries *et al.* and the Reed *et al.* studies were not able to refer to a record of their previous moves, unlike the procedure outlined above. Is this methodological difference likely to affect your results? In discussion, you might like to consider the implications of the phrase *learning by experience*. Do we learn strategies?

Alternatives

It would be fun to set up this experiment on a computer, testing out different ways of presenting information to subjects individually. Even without a computer, you could still test individually, perhaps giving subjects coins or models to move, as Reed *et al.* did, rather than asking them to write down their solution steps. For both of these alternatives you might specifically investigate the effects on learning of subjects being able to look back over a record of their moves, versus having to rely on memory for this review. Another advantage of individual testing is that you could record subjects' comments on their strategies as they solve the problems.

Reed *et al.* found that subjects failed to notice or make use of the fact that two problems were analogous, unless they were specifically alerted to the relationship between the problems. This is fairly surprising given that the structure of Missionaries and Cannibals is very close to Jealous Husbands and Wives, and suggests that more consideration needs to be given to determining the nature of analogies and their use in problem-solving situations. Gick and Holyoak (1980) presented a stimulating theoretical discussion on this topic. They were particularly interested in whether or not subjects were able to make a more general use of analogies to solve problems where the structure of the problems differed considerably. You could follow up their second experiment in which they looked at the extent of transfer for problems with different degrees of analogy.

Concentrating on problems that were more ill-defined than Missionaries and Cannibals, Gick and Holyoak devised several experiments to determine the specific features of two problems that need to be similar for subjects to recognise and use the relationship. You could replicate any of their experiments or investigate some of the suggestions they made about our everyday use of analogies in problem-solving.

It is interesting to note that Gick and Holyoak found more transfer between analogous problems when subjects were given the correct solution to one problem and had this available while they solved the other (Experiments 1 and 2), than when they had to generate the solutions to both problems (Experiment 3). Perhaps you could introduce this manipulation into the experiment of Reed *et al*. If subjects are provided the flow chart illustrating the solution steps for Missionaries and Cannibals, are they better able to make use of the analogy between that problem and Jealous Husbands and Wives?

When subjects are given solutions to similar problems or specific clues about analogies, we would expect them to make some attempt to use this information when solving a problem. But what happens in the everyday context where these hints are not usually available? Gick and Holyoak tried to simulate this situation in their Experiments 4 and 5. What implications do their results have for the design of courses to train people to be more efficient problem-solvers, for example in management or personnel administration contexts? You might like to construct some problems and analogies of your own, perhaps consulting some management training exercises.

References

Jeffries, R., Polson, P. G., Razran, L., and Atwood, M. E. A process model for Missionaries–Cannibals and other river-crossing problems. *Cognitive Psychology*, 1977, **9**, 412-40.

Reed, S. K., Ernst, G. W., and Banerji, R. The role of analogy in transfer between similar problem states. *Cognitive Psychology*, 1974, **6**, 436-50.

Reference for Alternatives

Gick, M. L., and Holyoak, K. J. Analogical problem solving. *Cognitive Psychology*, 1980, **12**, 306-55.

T6 Creativity

A talent reserved for some or a skill possessed by all?

The stage is set for a debate on the definition and criteria of 'creativity' by the question that heads this workshop. Frequently such debates centre on the particular characteristics of a creative product or person, with the implication that the talent is reserved for the few. Empirical research flowing from this standpoint is concerned with establishing a distinction between intelligence and creativity, or in demonstrating the relationship between a particular profile of personality traits and creative production (Dellas and Gaier, 1970).

The alternative standpoint sees creativity as a skill we all have in varying degrees and which can be measured by creativity tests. However, the validity of these tests is frequently questioned. Nicholls (1972), for example, argued that although the assumption underlying such tests is that creativity is a normally distributed trait, it is unlikely that high scorers on the tests will ever produce something that could be rated as creative. Perhaps creativity tests would be better described as measures of divergent thinking.

Differential performance on a pen-and-pencil creativity test or on a problem-solving task may not indicate differences in creativity, but rather differences in strategies employed, or in perception of task requirements. Indeed Nicholls suggested that creativity is situationally specific rather than a general trait.

De Bono (1970) would agree that everyone has the potential for divergent or lateral thought. According to him we need only to be aware of habitual thought strategies, and employ the unconventional. Given these proposals, we might ask whether environmental factors, such as special instructions or a particular atmosphere, would alter scores on a test of creativity.

Two main approaches to this question are set out below. It is suggested that you attempt just one of these. The first tests the hypothesis (Ziv, 1976) that 'laughter has a liberating effect on the flow of ideas' (p. 319). The second examines the effect on performance of specific instructions to think laterally.

Both approaches require the use of two forms of an open-ended creativity task, for example, Torrance's 'Unusual uses' for (a) tin cans and (b) cardboard boxes. Ideally the studies should be carried out over two sessions separated by a week, so that there is a suitable period between the administration of Form A of the task, and Form B, although our experience suggests that the two tests can be separated by as little as 40 minutes.

General procedure

The first study follows the procedure outlined by Ziv (1976). You will need two forms of a creativity task and a humorous record or tape recording. For our purposes, it is sufficient to run subjects in two groups, rather than Ziv's four-group design. Both groups complete Form A of the creativity task in the first session. In session two, the experimental group listens to the humorous record, then completes Form B. The control group simply completes Form B. Some thought needs to be given to establishing a relaxed and humorous atmosphere for the experimental group – one conducive to laughter.

You will need to compare the performance of each group on Form A and Form B, to determine the differences between conditions. Your main interest will be in the changes in performance from Form A to Form B. Is there a greater change in the experimental group's scores than in the control group's, regardless of the initial levels of creativity?

The scoring procedure will be largely determined by the creative task used and the availability of a scoring manual. However, even without a manual, it is fairly easy to give scores for fluency, flexibility and originality. For *fluency*, count the number of ideas; for *flexibility*, count the number of categories into which the ideas fall (for example, in the Torrance 'tin can' task some of the categories are: container, communication, flotation, furniture, support, wheel); and for *originality* you will need to determine the relative uniqueness of each subject's ideas. This may involve using a three-point scale of uniqueness based on how many subjects gave each response. Once you have determined for each idea how unique it is, you can give each subject a mean originality score, by averaging across his or her ideas.

The problems encountered when scoring, with or without a manual, could be raised in discussion, and linked to a general consideration of the criteria for creativity. You could also consider why laughter might increase creativity. Were your results normally distributed or did your subjects in each condition fall into two groups, high versus low scorers? Do those subjects who gained high scores perceive themselves as creative? You might ask subjects to talk about the strategies they used to generate ideas for the task.

Alternatives

You might decide to be more creative in (a) your choice of task, for example, use a drawing task or one that asks subjects to make up 'plot titles', or (b) the way in which you establish a humorous atmosphere. Extra time could be devoted to assessing the merits of the humorous record. Do subjects find it funny? Some attention might be given to linking the sort of humour contained on the record, to the ideas called for on the task (for example, *double entendre* with a plot title task). As well, you might consider the influence of the physical test situation. Should you use a classroom setting, or try more casual seating arrangements?

If you have a suitable number of subjects available, you could replicate Ziv's study in full, using the four-group Solomon design, to separate the effects of practice from the effects of humour.

The study of lateral thinking follows the General procedure discussed earlier. Two groups of subjects complete Forms A and B of a creativity task. This time, however, the experimental group are given special instructions in de Bono's techniques of lateral thinking before they complete Form B. The control group do not receive any special instructions.

The experimental instructions will need to be quite detailed, and should be printed for each subject. You could use the ideas that follow as a framework.

De Bono (1970) wrote '. . . the most basic principle of lateral thinking is that any particular way of looking at things is only one from among many other possible ways'. Thus when faced with a problem, he advises subjects to:

1 escape from cliches, list alternative uses, etc.;
2 challenge conventional assumptions;
3 list the functions, qualities and features of the object/problem, then use these as cues to new ideas;
4 restructure the problem; break the item into smaller units.

Provide an example to make these hints clearer. Try outlining all the uses for grass clippings, for instance. Begin by listing the properties of clippings when they are . . . dry, wet, set alight, packed, etc. From here, generate the uses that might be made of clippings in those states.

Consult the appropriate section in General procedure for details on scoring. Again you will need to compare the performance of each group on Form A and Form B to determine the relative differences.

In discussion, you could consider the problems that arise in scoring and examine the more general question 'Is lateral thinking the same as creative thinking?'

References

De Bono, E. *Lateral Thinking: A Textbook in Creativity*. London: Ward Lock Educational, 1970.
Dellas, M., and Gaier, E. L. Identification of creativity: The individual. *Psychological Bulletin*, 1970, **73**, 55-73.

170   *Thinking*

Nicholls, J. G. Creativity in the person who will never produce anything original and useful: The concept of creativity as a normally distributed trait. *American Psychologist*, 1972, **27**, 717–26.
Ziv, A. Facilitating effects of humor on creativity. *Journal of Educational Psychology*, 1976, **68**, 318–22.

T7 Decision-making strategies
Thinking in a social context

In everyday use we often attach the term 'thinking' to statements about our beliefs, interests, decisions and feelings of mental effort. This intuition about the business of thinking does not always match research in the area. Within cognitive processes, the study of thinking has typically been confined to processes involved in the solution of ingenious artificial problems rather than real-life problems. Cognitive researchers have seldom dealt with social problem-solving.

Thinking in a social context is likely to be influenced by an individual's personal beliefs and by interaction with the views of others. Social psychologists have studied these aspects of thinking under the guise of attitude formation, persuasion and group decision processes. They have, however, paid more attention to the outcome of thinking than to the processes.

A possible meeting ground between social and cognitive psychologists lies in studying the processes involved in making everyday decisions. Even here it is difficult to investigate these decisions, because in order to describe the processes involved in a particular decision we need to take account of the decision-maker's background knowledge and views on the relevant issues.

Another difficulty is that everyday decisions are often based on a best guess, perhaps because our knowledge is incomplete, or because we need to make a prediction about future events. We know little about the strategies used to make such best guesses, apart from the work of Tversky and Kahneman (1974), who described common heuristic strategies, including 'representativeness' and 'availability'. They suggested that in making a decision about the probability of A (e.g. the tall, good-looking person at a party) belonging to a particular category B (e.g. model), we tend to rely on a judgment about the 'representativeness' or similarity of A to our stereotype of B, and to ignore information about the true probability that A is likely to belong to B (i.e. there are relatively few models). Moreover, judgments about the probability of an event occurring in the future (e.g. will John become a star?), are biased by the ease with which we can either recall a similar instance from our past experience or construct a plausible scenario leading up to that event (e.g. John is appearing in a play and a top producer is coming to watch). That is, the judgment is biased by the 'availability' of relevant information in memory.

The effects of these two heuristic strategies are difficult to separate in complex social decisions, because category stereotypes are probably most readily available in memory. Try remembering a real-estate agent that you have met, for instance. The task remains to determine how category stereotypes and other factors influence the relative availability of information in everyday decision contexts.

Reyes, Thompson and Bower (1980) have begun to do this for the sorts of decisions made in courtroom settings. They were interested in investigating variables that affect the memorability of relevant information over time, and how differences in the availability of material reflect jurors' attitudes and influence their subsequent decisions about guilt. Subjects were given a series of arguments for and against a defendant in a drunk driving case. The two variables that Reyes *et al*. hypothesised would differentially influence the memorability of these arguments and hence affect decisions were (a) vividness of the arguments and (b) character of the defendant: good guy versus bad guy. More vivid arguments should be better remembered, and our stereotypes about the behaviour of a good guy as opposed to a bad guy, should bias our expectations of guilt leading to selective recall of the evidence. In support of their predictions, they found subjects were more likely to remember vividly presented arguments and to recall unfavourable information about the good guy and favourable information about the bad guy. These factors especially influenced judgments made after a delay. It seems from their results that if you are taken to court on a drunk driving charge, you should present yourself as a bad guy, offer a vivid defence, and seek an adjournment before the verdict is decided!

This workshop is a partial replication of Reyes *et al*. and asks two questions: what are the effects of information regarding a defendant's character on the judged importance of and memory for evidence, and what is the relationship between the availability of information and the judgment of guilt? To avoid the possible confounding present in Reyes *et al*. resulting from subjects making two judgments, and from only testing delayed recall, subjects in this study will be asked to recall regardless of delay and each subject will make only one judgment of guilt.

General procedure

You will need to decide the number of variables that you can efficiently manipulate in this study, with a final choice taking account of your available time and subject numbers. If you are limited to one testing session and a small number of subjects, you could have a two-group design varying only the defendant's character (e.g. good guy versus bad guy), and have all subjects make a judgment after a short delay, say 40 minutes. With a larger subject pool and/or two test sessions you could introduce additional defendant groups, factorially combine defendant's character and vividness of arguments, extend the delay prior to final judgment, or compare immediate versus delayed judgments.

Having settled your design, the next step is the construction of a plausible transcript of a court case. You could simply follow the ideas given by Reyes *et al.* and create a basic drunk driving case which could involve any type of defendant, or construct a case involving a different crime, using the same format.

Reyes *et al.*'s transcript consisted of a 150-word statement of background information to the case, a short pen-portrait of the defendant, nine arguments attributed to the defence and nine to the prosecution. The defence and prosecution arguments should be the same, regardless of your choice of type of defendant. If you are not manipulating the vividness of these arguments, then this factor should also be controlled to avoid drawing attention to a particular argument. Some pilot testing would be worthwhile here, perhaps using subjects' ratings to control the impact of the arguments across types of defendants.

You will need to decide the character of your defendants. Reyes *et al.* gave their description of a good guy versus a bad guy but seem not to have collected data on how representative their descriptions were of the common category stereotypes for these character types. The representativeness of the description may affect its subsequent availability. Controlling for representativeness would be an interesting and worthwhile addition to your study. You could simply get some independent subjects to write a pen-portrait of a good guy and a bad guy for example, and use the most frequent ideas to construct your description of a typical good guy and a typical bad guy. Collecting these data might also provide some insight into the differential importance placed on some aspects of the evidence depending on the defendant's character.

The transcripts and defendant descriptions can be presented to subjects in booklet form, allowing you to test all subjects together. Following Reyes *et al.* you should probably have one argument per page and keep the order of argument presentation the same for all subjects, as would be the case in an ordinary court setting. Rather than presenting subjects with the description of the defendant after an outline of the case following Reyes *et al.*, it is probably better to give them the description first, since this ordering has been found in other memory experiments to have a greater impact: it gives subjects a specific framework for considering the defendant's case right from the start.

Subjects read through their transcript booklet, then are asked to rate the importance of each of the arguments on a scale ranging from strong support for the defence to strong support for the prosecution. After a delay, subjects attempt to recall the arguments previously presented, indicating the importance of these arguments for the defendant's defence or prosecution. Reyes *et al.* re-presented the original 18 arguments for this second opinion.

However, it could be argued that asking subjects to rate just those arguments that they recall provides a more accurate measure of relative importance.

The next step is to have subjects make a decision about the defendant's guilt. Reyes *et al.* asked their subjects to indicate on three 11-point scales, (a) their personal judgment, (b) the decision they would make if they were on a jury, and (c) a judgment about the extent to which the defendant was drunk. They subsequently averaged these responses. For ease of comparison, you could adopt their scales and questions. However, because they found a high correlation between their scales, you could simply give subjects one scale and have them judge degree of guilt. You might include some further questions at the end, asking subjects about the strategy they used to make their decision and why they rated some arguments as more important than others.

The data from each subject will consist of two importance scores for each argument, the number and type of arguments recalled, and a judgment of guilt. As well, Reyes *et al.* combined the ratio of prosecution to defence arguments recalled and the relative importance given to these arguments into a relative strength index for each subject (pp. 7–8). You can compare the treatment groups in your study on each of these dependent variables. If you are not familiar with analysis of variance, you need only report means and standard deviations, or use *t*-tests to assess significant differences. You could also present scatter plots to illustrate any correlations between the type of arguments recalled and judged degree of guilt, and between the relative strength index and judged guilt.

Do your results correspond to those of Reyes *et al.*? Did the factors that you introduced to manipulate the availability of information have a significant effect on subjects' recall and judgments of guilt? Were subjects more likely to recall arguments that were incongruent with the descriptions of the defendant? You could discuss any comments your subjects made about their decisions and any implications your results have for the principle that a defendant is innocent until proven guilty. You might also consider the general use of Tversky and Kahneman's heuristic strategies, and their function in decision-making. In what other ways could we manipulate the availability of particular information and how could we determine the stereotypes that subjects are likely to use when making judgments based on a representativeness strategy?

Alternatives

There are several alternatives that have already been mentioned for this workshop which you might consider if you have additional time and subjects available. You could consider changing the type of crime, to test the generality of Reyes *et al.*'s results. It may be that the sort of information used to make a judgment about a drunk driving offence in which no other person was injured will be different from that used when further complications are introduced to the case (e.g. a passenger is killed) or when the nature of the crime changes (for example to a bank robbery or a rape case). Here you would need to consider the stereotypes we hold about both the defendant and the victim. Again, it would be useful in constructing your hypothetical case, to have an independent group of subjects fill out the story behind the case and indicate their attitude toward the defendant and the victim. You could also examine to what extent availability is influenced by the credibility of the witness presenting the evidence to the court.

A useful, but time-consuming, technique from the problem-solving literature would be to have subjects 'think aloud' as they make their decisions. Analysis of subject protocols could provide some interesting information about the steps involved in subjects' final judgments.

You could replicate any of the experiments demonstrating the effects of the representativeness or availability strategies on decision-making, described by Tversky and Kahneman, perhaps extending them to more real-life settings, as Snyder and Cantor (1979) have done. They found that, when subjects were asked to judge the suitability of an applicant for a particular job, they tended differentially to recall those features of the candidate's history which were appropriate to their perception of the type of job, rather than those which were inappropriate — a combination of the availability and representativeness strategies. They also found that subjects adopted a strategy of collecting evidence to confirm rather than to refute their impressions. You could replicate any of their studies, perhaps changing the type of jobs and the personality styles of the applicants. You could also consider providing subjects with the histories of two or more applicants for the one position, to see what effect this has on the confirmation strategy. You might consider other settings which require judgments on contradictory evidence (e.g. the stock market) and investigate the type of decision processes that operate there. In what contexts do we select information that confirms our hypotheses or best guesses based on stereotypes, rather than searching for alternatives?

The studies so far have concentrated on decisions made about people. In a social setting however, we also make decisions about the likelihood of particular events. Slovic, Fischhoff and Lichtenstein (1976) noted the importance of these sorts of decisions and described several studies in which subjects were asked to judge things like the frequency of particular causes of death, or the occurrence of natural disasters. As in the other studies mentioned in this workshop, they also found consistent biases for these types of judgments. The advantage of their studies is that they do not rely on subjects having to learn a new set of information before making a decision. If you decide to follow up any of the studies they mentioned (e.g. judgments about the causes of death), you should compare your subjects' estimates to the relevant statistics for your country.

176   *Thinking*

References

Reyes, R. M., Thompson, W. C., and Bower, G. H. Judgmental biases resulting from differing availabilities of arguments. *Journal of Personality and Social Psychology*, 1980, **39**, 2-12.

Tversky, A., and Kahneman, D. Judgment under uncertainty: Heuristics and biases. *Science*, 1974, **185**, 1124-31. Also in P. N. Johnson-Laird and P. C. Wason (eds). *Thinking: Readings in Cognitive Science.* Cambridge: Cambridge University Press, 1977.

References for Alternatives

Snyder, M., and Cantor, N. Testing hypotheses about people: The use of historical knowledge. *Journal of Experimental Social Psychology*, 1979, **15**, 330-42.

Slovic, P., Fischhoff, B., and Lichtenstein, S. Cognitive processes in societal risk taking. In J. S. Carroll and J. W. Payne (eds). *Cognition and Social Behavior*. Hillsdale, New Jersey: Lawrence Erlbaum Associates, 1976.